GOD
I QUIT

Christian J. Ramirez

WESTBOW
PRESS®
A DIVISION OF THOMAS NELSON
& ZONDERVAN

WestBow Press books may be ordered through booksellers or by contacting:

WestBow Press
A Division of Thomas Nelson & Zondervan
1663 Liberty Drive
Bloomington, IN 47403
www.westbowpress.com
844-714-3454

ISBN: 978-1-6642-9483-7 (sc)
ISBN: 978-1-6642-9596-4 (hc)
ISBN: 978-1-6642-9484-4 (e)

Library of Congress Control Number: 2023904502

Print information available on the last page.

WestBow Press rev. date: 3/22/2023

ABOUT THE AUTHOR

Christian Ramirez is married to his best friend Delila, and Father to 3 smart amazing kids. He is a Marine Corps Veteran, former Diesel Heavy Equipment Technician, former Real Estate Agent, and now Author. Calls Southern California home. Oh yea, he never got a College Degree, never even graduated High School, yet look where God has taken him. All glory to God!

CHAPTER 1

You Have My Undivided Attention (Marriage Testimony)

LET'S GET STRAIGHT TO IT. THIS EVENT IS WHAT CHANGED MY LIFE forever. I got to the point in my life where I continued to do what I thought was right in God's eyes, but I was doing it alone. I was making bad choices and I wasn't going anywhere. I wasn't going to God to work through the consequences I rightfully earned. I just didn't face them, but cowardly lied and lied, to try to escape my sin while consciously sinning. I believed in God. I believed in His Son, Jesus Christ, but I still had myself in the front seat, never completely surrendering.

I lived my life as a "Christian". I read my bible once in a while. I went to Church on Sundays...sometimes. Ok fine, when I had time for it, which was seldom. Prayed here and there. I tried to be a good person, and do the things Jesus taught us to do and be. I still cussed here and there. I watched what the secular world watched. I listened to what the secular world listened to. I liked to drink to have a good time. I wasn't an alcoholic or anything or did any drugs. Being the best example of a Father I can be, and even tithed my 10% as often as I could. I thought I was a decent person, saved by the cross of Jesus Christ. I mean I'm only human, I'm going to make a mistake once in a while. Until one night...everything changed.

I'm driving on the freeway, westbound towards LA. It was 10 o' clock at night. My eyes filled with tears, barely able to see the road in front of me. I'm taking deep breaths as I cry out to my Father in heaven, "God, what have I done!?"

Hours earlier...my wife and I were having a deep discussion about the past and she tells me she believes God is telling her there's something to be said. I finally confess that 4 years ago, I kissed another woman. Of course she's very upset and hurt, and asks if there's anything else, and I of course, say no.

But God encourages her to seek for more information. Like there's more I need to tell her. She continues to press on asking, "So you haven't done anything else with any other woman?" As always, I told her, "No, I haven't done anything else. You're out of your mind to think that." But her discernment is strong and God isn't going to let it go this time. I feel this tightness around my throat, I can barely breathe. I'm sitting on the ground looking at my toddlers lying peacefully in their small bed. As I put my hands on their small backs, I begin to imagine and say to myself, "If I tell her the truth, I may not have this moment with them again as I am now. I will lose them. I will not be able to be the Dad I've always wanted to be. I will lose my wife, my best friend. She will leave me and everything will crumble... because of me. If I continue to lie and keep this deep dark secret, we can stay married and I will continue to try and better myself just as I have been trying." My neck is gripped tighter. I began to tear up, feeling my family slipping away because of MY actions.

At this point, I can't breathe, it's hard to swallow. I have never felt this before. It was undoubtedly supernatural. I tell my wife, "Ok, let's talk in the living room." We are looking into each other's eyes and she says, "Look, let's put our rings on top of the ottoman and lay it all down, once and for all, and put it behind us." I'm hesitating, but I still have difficulty breathing. God is not letting me get away this time. Then I tell her, "5 years ago, I committed adultery."

Immediately, her heart broke. With tears in her eyes, she asks me why I did it, who it was with, how it happened, then she kicks me out. I get in my truck. She is broken and I'm rightfully out of the house. God revealed the truth and now I'm getting what is coming to me. I don't know where to go or what to do. I drive but with nowhere to go. I call my brother, he doesn't answer. Only other person I know who would allow me to stay at their place is my cousin near LA. I call her and she answers. I tell her what happened, disappointedly she tells me what was I thinking and to come over. I begin to drive westbound on the freeway. I continue my prayer in complete disappointment in myself,

"God…You have my full undivided attention. I am a horrible Husband and Father. How could I have let this happen? Whatever You want me to do, I'll do it. I'm sorry for what I have done. I give You my life. No matter what happens next, I will trust You. I've been doing it my way and look where it took me. I know You are God and I will put my trust in You alone. God please take over. I'm all in. No more saying that You're my God but not acting like it. I will devote my life to You fully and surrender fully. I'm repenting from my life of doing things my way. I'm done with the results I've been getting. No matter how hard I've tried, it didn't get anywhere. I'm sick and tired of being sick and tired. So God… I quit. I'm done doing things without You. I'm all Yours. Whatever consequences I may face, I accept them today. I'm sorry for my choices. I take full responsibility. Father, I know You are a just God and will do what must be done. If my kids are taken away, please help me through it. I don't deserve her. I will be a better Father than I was a Husband. Thank You Lord for never leaving me. In Jesus name I pray…Amen."

And when I said this, my life changed. My mind was set. I didn't care what happened to me next, I deserved the worst. I believe God tested my words to see if what I said was genuine or if I was just having a moment of defeat and guilt that day. He began to make me right the wrongs I've committed. I had to fight for my marriage like never before. If I wanted this marriage to continue, I had to put my pride aside and be the Husband I was supposed to be and more. I fell to my knees many times after this, asking for help, patience, and strength. I wasn't alone anymore, I had God. This time for real. He helped me every step of the way.

The only reason she didn't divorce me that day, was because she felt God wanted her to rebuild and she was being obedient to God. With all of her being, she wanted out and rightfully so. And many times after that, she asks God if there was another way without me in the picture. But I believe God was there and He was the only reason we continued to work at this marriage.

The next few years were brutal. And because I'm human, I still got impatient and frustrated. But thank the merciful and graceful God, who was continuously working on me and in me. I had thoughts from the enemy, telling me it would be easier to start over with another person, than work on this marriage which I had broken. This is where my flesh was weak but my spirit was willing. I wanted to do everything I could to make it work. I even asked God to kill me if it meant a better life for her and the kids, but God obviously had other plans. He knew how He would transform this selfish weak pathetic coward into a selfless, bold, loving warrior for His kingdom. He knew He was going to change my heart and mind. He picked me up from my lowest point in my life. He was always there, it was I, who rejected His hands of mercy and grace.

Some parts of my character changed immediately. My demeanor changed towards marriage. Our discussions changed. My patience grew. And so did my relationship with God. I begin to go to Him for everything. I learned if I focus on Him first, my marriage, my parenting, my friendships, and more, are going to be more than fine, they will be blessed beyond measure.

Fast forward to 2022, my wife and I are stronger than ever. Trust continues to build, but EVERYTHING else is better than before the day the Holy Spirit had me in that headlock (or if a demon tried stopping me from speaking the truth I've been hiding, still don't know exactly what happened that night). I love her more than ever. I'm telling you, it gets really good. We talk about everything, and there are no secrets in our lives. It truly feels free to have all the truth out. Of course it's a whole other story with how she feels, the hurt, the pain, the rejection, and having to look at me every single day and remember what I did. But everyday, with Jesus Christ, she chooses to forgive me. She sees God is good and what progress God has done to me and continues to do in me.

I don't deserve my wife. I don't deserve my children. I don't deserve my life. But through Christ, it has become possible. I wake up grateful and feeling like I'm in this dream where everything is working for God's glory and honor, and that's my heart's desire. God is so good. I feel like I'm 1000% ahead of where I should be, where I deserve to be. So when I run into a problem or a struggle in my life, it may feel like a punishment for my past mistakes and brings me down a bit. But I also feel like every blessing I receive pushes me forward. Nothing could ever counter what God has done for me. Nothing will phase the faith I have in my Father who has delivered me. I will always and forever be God's, and He will direct my path. I live for Him now!

This is our marriage testimony. From this, many other ventures were born. We have our house testimony in the middle of the real estate chaos. God still does miracles and we're separate from what the world goes through. He takes care of His children.

Spirit of Anger

During this marriage restoration process, I continued to overcome my anger issues. I grew up punching walls and brought this into my marriage. I never hit my wife but I hit walls, doors, concrete, metal, and wooden frames. But as I asked God for patience and peace, I was released from this hold that anger and wrath had over me. I still get upset at times but it isn't at the level it once was. As God continues to work on me and I come into agreement with Him, I am allowing the Holy Spirit to grow good fruit in my life and prune the bad ones. I want to continue fighting against these spirits and ensure I'm delivered from this.

As I read the word about anger and being patient, this is what comes up and helps me overcome difficult moments. Understanding what God wants me to do and how to act. Mentioning that we should walk in humility, kindness, gentle but put away wrath, clamor, evil speaking and endure hardships, beatings, imprisonment, persecution, hunger, and more. This isn't easy but it is commendable to God. We need Him, in order to endure all this and overcome it. It's easy to become offended and react impulsively, but it leads to sin which gives birth to death and invites all sorts of evil into our lives.

"The discretion of a man makes him slow to anger, And his glory is to overlook a transgression."
Proverbs 19:11 NKJV

"A person's wisdom yields patience; it is to one's glory to overlook an offense."
Proverbs 19:11 NIV

"He who is slow to anger is better than the mighty, And he who rules his spirit than he who takes a city."
Proverbs 16:32 NKJV

"Let all bitterness, wrath, anger, clamor, and evil speaking be put away from you, with all malice."
Ephesians 4:31 NKJV

"Remind them to be subject to rulers and authorities, to obey, to be ready for every good work, to speak evil of no one, to be peaceable, gentle, showing all humility to all men."
Titus 3:1-2 NKJV

"...as servants of God we commend ourselves in every way: in <u>great endurance</u>; in troubles, hardships and distresses; in beatings, imprisonments and riots; in hard work, sleepless nights and hunger; in purity, understanding, <u>patience</u> and <u>kindness</u>; in the Holy Spirit and in sincere love;"
2 Corinthians 6:4-6 NIV

"strengthened with all might, according to His glorious power, for all <u>patience</u> and <u>longsuffering</u> with joy"
Colossians 1:11 NKJV

"Therefore, as the elect of God, holy and beloved, put on tender mercies, <u>kindness</u>, <u>humility</u>, meekness, <u>longsuffering (patience)</u>; bearing with one another, and <u>forgiving one another</u>, if anyone has a complaint against another; even as Christ forgave you, so you also must do.
Colossians 3:12-13 NKJV

"Preach the word! Be ready in season and out of season. Convince, rebuke, exhort, with all <u>longsuffering</u> and teaching."
2 Timothy 4:2 NKJV

"But <u>avoid foolish and ignorant disputes</u>, knowing that they generate strife. And a servant of the Lord must not quarrel but <u>be gentle to all</u>, able to teach, <u>patient</u>, in <u>humility</u> correcting those who are in opposition, if God perhaps will grant them repentance, so that they may know the truth,"
2 Timothy 2:23-25 NKJV

"not lagging in diligence, fervent in spirit, serving the Lord; rejoicing in hope, <u>patient</u> in tribulation, continuing steadfastly in prayer; distributing to the needs of the saints, given to hospitality."
Romans 12:11-13 NKJV

So if you know what true anger and wrath feels like, then you are most likely battling against this spirit. Yes, you may feel powerful to have this anger inside, heating you up, giving you strength in the middle of the injustice that is happening to you or around you. But I can tell you, it is a lie.

This vengeful feeling isn't helping you release tension and stress. It's hurting you. It's scientifically proven that angry people are 19% more likely than calmer people to get a heart disease. Especially those of us who tighten our fists and burst our blood vessels in my chest, neck and eyes from so much intensity. I used to scare kids when they say the blood in my eyes. I looked like a demon to them. And this made me feel inferior and nobody wanted to mess with me. Our increased blood pressure that breaks through our vessels are indicators that there is TOO MUCH pressure in our system and our hearts are paying for it. You are destroying your heart and brain. You are letting that person or situation overcome you but getting you upset. To this day, I'm glad no one ever pushed me to the point where I snapped and physically acted upon it. I would have killed someone. I would have unleashed all the anger I built up inside over all those years. All the hurt and pain I held, I would've made that one person feel all the pain I wanted to give to all those other people have caused me and more.

I say all this to say, there is freedom from this slavery of anger. You can finally have self- control. To actually brush off the offense and walk confidently in knowing who you are and what you're capable of. To finally not let other people's opinions or actions dictate your actions and emotions. Such freedom you have never felt before. Ask God today to remove this from you.

Try it. Say, "I renounce all the pain I've spoken over others. I will no longer give them power over me. I forgive everyone who has ever hurt me, and release this hold over me from this day forward. God, please help me mean this and continue to forgive them even though they don't deserve it. Help me regain my self-control and exceed in it. Allow me to feel Your peace and forgiveness. I speak this in Jesus name. Amen." When you say this with all of your heart and mean it, you WILL feel God's holy power over you. You will begin to feel weight fall off of you. You will know what true peace is. Nothing will phase you. Someone will try to offend you and it won't strike a chord like it used to, and you will notice it and be glad that it doesn't control you anymore. Joy then comes. No matter your circumstance, God will reveal His joy and love in Your heart.

As time goes on, you'll learn to love and have compassion even on those who deliberately come after you and your family. This is when you'll know you have reached a level with God and understand why He sent His precious and only Son for us. You will finally understand His heart and why He wants us to love each other.

Spirit of Lust & Porn

God also helped me get delivered from lust addiction. I was introduced to porn at age 5, when an older boy showed me some pictures in a magazine. From that point forward, I struggled with lust. Looking at girls with perverted eyes. Really started watching porn at age 11, and continued throughout High School and into the Marine Corps. In the military, it was worse. We would trade videos and encourage each other to embrace it. Singling out those who didn't watch them. When I got married, I thought it would just stop. I was completely wrong. As the bible says, to look at a woman lustfully is committing adultery.

"But I say to you that whoever looks at a woman to <u>lust</u> for her has already committed adultery with her in his heart."
Matthew 5:28 NKJV

I was in bondage and I wasn't repenting. After my greatest secret was revealed, I really tried to stop. I prayed for it to stop and was disgusted with myself when I did it. I knew the Holy Spirit was convicting me because I felt horrible just by thinking about it.

One day, I got home early. I was alone and I wanted to watch a movie or get some errands done. But a voice whispers in my ear,

"Let's watch something." I've always heard these whispers, but I always thought it was me; my perverted fleshly mind. This time I recognized it wasn't me. These weren't my thoughts because I really didn't want to do it. But this time, I fought back. I yelled in my empty house, "Get away from me! I never want to watch porn again!" I felt these whispers leave. I felt free. I began to pray, "God help me. You know I've been struggling to stop. Search my heart. I don't want this to continue destroying my marriage and my walk with You. Help me not be lustful any longer. Help me have self-control."

From that point forward, I stopped hearing these whispers and temptations to porn. I was a slave to it but now I'm finally free. But be careful, just because you are freed from something, doesn't mean it's not going to try and get you back. I now have no thoughts of watching porn, but I still hear these voices from further back. Almost as if they were across the street from my house, calling for me, trying to tempt me. But I know they aren't from within me. So there is still temptation all around us but we need to choose to fight back and not give in. God won't simply take away temptation but will give us a way of escape and endurance to bear while we are still on this earth. We need to captivate our thoughts and put them in submission to Christ. And continue to ask God for help, and it gets easier as the enemy gets tired of trying, but nevertheless, they won't stop trying, so resist the devil.

The following verses teach us about temptation, bringing thoughts into captivity, resisting the devil, to not walk in revelry, lust, and envy but to walk in the Spirit.

"...God is faithful, who will not allow you to be tempted beyond what you are able, but with the <u>temptation</u> will also make the way of escape, that you may be able to bear it."
1 Corinthians 10:13 NKJV

"For though we walk in the flesh, we do not war according to the flesh. For the weapons of our warfare are not carnal but mighty in God for pulling down strongholds, casting down arguments and every high thing that exalts itself against the knowledge of God, <u>bringing every thought into captivity to the obedience of Christ</u>,"
2 Corinthians 10:3-5 NKJV

"Therefore <u>submit to God</u>. <u>Resist the devil</u> and he will flee from you."
James 4:7 NKJV

"Let us walk properly, as in the day, not in revelry and drunkenness, not in lewdness and <u>lust</u>, not in strife and envy."
Romans 13:13 NKJV

"I say then: Walk in the Spirit, and you shall not fulfill the <u>lust</u> of the flesh. For the flesh <u>lusts</u> against the Spirit, and the Spirit against the flesh; and these are contrary to one another, so that you do not do the things that you wish."
Galatians 5:16-17 NKJV

"And you He made alive, who were dead in trespasses and sins, in which... we all once conducted ourselves in the <u>lusts</u> of our flesh, fulfilling the desires of the flesh and of the mind, and were by nature children of wrath, just as the others."
Ephesians 2:1-2,3 NKJV

"Flee also youthful <u>lusts</u>; but pursue righteousness, faith, love, peace with those who call on the Lord out of a pure heart."
2 Timothy 2:22 NKJV

"For the grace of God that brings salvation has appeared to all men, teaching us that, denying ungodliness and worldly <u>lusts</u>, we should live soberly, righteously, and godly in the present age,"
Titus 2:11-12

"...the world (and its things) is passing away, and the <u>lust</u> of it; but he who does the will of God abides forever."
1 John 2:17 NKJV

Spirit of Lying & Deceit

Also during this restoration season, God helped me not to lie anymore. I understood I would pile up lie after lie, in order to cover up the truth. I was a pathological liar. I would lie about everything. To make myself look better than others, and to get away from my consequences. God hates a lying tongue. His Word says,

"<u>Lying lips</u> are an abomination to the Lord, But those who deal truthfully are His delight."
Proverbs 12:22 NKJV

I even lied to myself, thinking I was a good person. I could lie and it didn't affect me. I knew the bible said God despises a lying tongue but I didn't know how to stop. When my secret was revealed, and I finally fully surrendered to God, something broke off of me. I never wanted to lie again. I liked this freedom I felt. And I don't want to disappoint my heavenly Father anymore.

So I just said it in my heart, "I will no longer lie." The Holy Spirit has placed this in my heart and I can't lie anymore. I will always tell the truth. I won't say I did something if I didn't actually do it. I won't ever put a checkmark in a box that I didn't perform. I'll just tell the truth. If it puts me in a bind, then oh well, as long as I'm not displeasing my God, I'm good. If I get persecuted for speaking the truth, then so be it. If my job wants me to lie about something, I'll simply tell them, "I can't and won't do that." If I get fired, oh well.

Now there is a difference between speaking the truth with condemnation and speaking the truth with love, and possibly tough love. If you know someone who is sinning, and want to tell them they should stop, we need God's help on how we should go about it.

When I read the word about practicing falsehood and lying, it also says:

"Blessed are those who do His commandments, that they may have the right to the tree of life, and may enter through the gates into the city. But outside are dogs and sorcerers and sexually immoral and murderers and idolaters, and whoever loves and practices a lie."
Revelation 22:14-15 NKJV

"But the cowardly, unbelieving, abominable, murderers, sexually immoral, sorcerers, idolaters, and all liars shall have their part in the lake which burns with fire and brimstone, which is the second death."
Revelation 21:8 ESV

"You are of your father the devil, and the desires of your father you want to do. He was a murderer from the beginning, and does not stand in the truth, because there is no truth in him. When he speaks a lie, he speaks from his own resources, for he is a liar and the father of it."
John 8:44 NKJV

I will not lie and deny the truth, for my God is the truth. He is my Father, not the devil. I will not be left outside with the dogs, sorcerers, sexually immoral, murderers, idolaters, in the lake of fire to burn for eternity. I will abide in the truth, which is Jesus Christ. Through Him I will have eternal life for He is the only way.

"Therefore, putting away lying, "Let each one of you speak truth with his neighbor," for we are members of one another."
Ephesians 4:29 NKJV

"...as servants of God we commend ourselves in every way:... in <u>truthful</u> <u>speech</u> and in the power of God; with weapons of righteousness in the right hand and in the left;"
2 Corinthians 6:4,7 NIV

Now let's get into my other testimonies, intense stories that God has helped me through and some Life Lessons that may help you clarify some issues in your life and walk with God.

CHAPTER 2

Are We Moving Again?

Before I get into our 2 homeownership testimonies. I would like to share my story of how it all led up to that point. Growing up in Southern California, I moved a lot. Like A LOT. I'll break it down.

Home #1: Pre-K
Home #2: K (not completing Kindergarten)
Home #3: K-3rd (not completing 3rd)
Home #4: 3rd (not completing 3rd)
Home #5: 3-4th
Home #6: 5-6th (not completing 6th)
Home #7: 6-8th
Home #8: 9-10th (not completing 10th)
Home #9: 10th
Home #10: 11-12th (not completing 12th)
Home #11: 12th (never completing 12th, never even graduating…)

This happened because we struggled financially. We would move to a home, live there for a bit, and when we couldn't afford it any longer, we would have to move to another home. They felt bad moving us from school to school, but they were in survival mode with 4 kids. I believe my Mother prayed for the next home we were able to afford and God always came through.

I remember in Home #4, being 8 years old and in 3rd grade; I told the kids at school, "There's no point in being friends. I'll probably move soon." And I wasn't wrong, we moved within 6 months.

Never Graduated

Now I never graduated High School, partially because we moved so much. One time I mentioned this to my family and to my surprise, my sister didn't know. And this was 11 years after the year I was supposed to graduate.

We just moved into a new city and I attended the nearby High School (Home #8). I was a freshman and I didn't know a SINGLE person, no friends, but thankfully I stayed there for the whole school year, and half of my sophomore year. Then my family finally found an opportunity to buy a house and moved in the middle of my sophomore year (Home #9). Which meant I had to attend a new High School. Here we go again.

I attended the new High School for 1 day and I witnessed security guards hanging out with students and from the looks of it, exchanging drugs. During the next week, I met my teachers. I realized most of them didn't care about the education of the students, or at least lost hope because of the undisciplined students who didn't care enough about their future. Some of the teachers gave out A's to those they liked and F's to those they didn't.

To all this, I realized I actually cared about my education and future. I wanted to leave this school and return to my previous one. But there were 2 problems. First of all, my parents couldn't drive me to my previous school, it was too far. My Dad went to work too early to take me, and my Mom had to take my brother to the school nearby.

Secondly, I was in a different school district. So it wasn't permitted for me to return. I wrote a letter to my old High School's Vice Principal. She outright rejected me.

As this really discouraged me, I still persisted to my Mother that I didn't want to return to the corrupted school. She then helped me enter independent study, which meant I would get a huge packet of homework, read all the textbooks on my own, and complete it within the next few weeks. I tried it for 2 days, and I decided I'm not going to do this. I might as well drop out of school now.

My lack of focus didn't allow me to finish any homework. I mean it when I say, I never did homework while in elementary school or in middle school, unless I was really interested in it. By this point, I haven't attended school for about 3 weeks now.

I then tried sending another letter, but this time to the Principal. I wrote stating my situation and what I was feeling about the other school. That I will do all that I could to get to school on my own and felt that his school's staff really cared about the students. And because of this, that's where I wanted to be. He accepted my request. I was so thrilled to return to school.

For the next 6-8 months, I would wake up at 5 AM and go to the city bus stop around 5:25 AM. The bus would pick me up at 5:30 AM and I would sit until the bus arrived at my school at 7:30 AM. Bell rang at 7:30 AM, so I ran to my first period every day. Of course I explained this to my teacher and they understood my minor tardiness.

Yet another thing came against me, my Vice Principal. She was so angry that I was able to return to her school, despite her rejection, she told me I wouldn't get my entire 1st Semester credits. For the 2nd Semester, I pushed myself to take extra classes to make up for any lost credits. I was never able to catch up.

Then the Real Estate Market crashed. We lost our home, this really upset us. We finally got into a house of our own after all these years and then this happened. So we moved (Home #10). I remained going to the same High School and I began my Junior year.

During the end of my Junior year, my counselor told me I

wouldn't get to graduate my Senior year, but suggested I take the CHSPE (California High School Proficiency Examination) test. And if I passed this test, I would be able to leave school early. I took the test and passed with flying colors. I was able to leave my Junior year of High School, but I decided to stay so that I can enjoy all the Senior activities. I wanted to go to Homecoming, Prom, Grad Night, and finally enter a sport.

And I did just that. I did all the things the Seniors did. I still did my best in my classes, completing Advanced Economy, Advanced Calculus (for 1 semester haha). I joined the Cross Country team and Track team. I was in the leadership class. I enjoyed my friends and what I was able to experience as a Senior. During this year, we moved once more as the Landlord decided to sell the house. We couldn't afford it after losing all of our savings from the last house we tried to buy. So Home #11 (the last house I lived in with my parents). I continued to drive to my high school, I wasn't going to let another move deter me from my high school. When graduation came, I didn't walk. Didn't receive my diploma. I was there, sitting in the stands while I saw all my friends walk down the aisle to receive what they've accomplished. I was short about 20 credits to graduate, but I did have my CHSPE certificate, just wished I would have walked with them. I met with them afterward, and we all attended grad night together. Most of them to this day, think I graduated because I was wearing my cap and gown that night.

Joining the Marine Corps

During my Senior year, I met with the Marine Corps recruiter and he said I should be able to go to boot camp a few months after the school year ends. When that time came around, we looked at the qualifications to enter the military, and that year, they weren't accepting GED or CHSPE certificates anymore. When he told me this news, I was very disappointed. I asked if there is anything I could do. He said, "The only other way is to get a certificate from an Adult School."

I went to my local Adult School and told them my situation. The counselor said it was impossible for what I needed. I needed 20 credits within 1 month, and each class worth 5 credits takes about 3 months to pass. Then, like if I was in a movie, he dramatically pauses, sighs and says quietly, "Look, they have these tests you can take. They are difficult but if you pass them, you can get instant credits. And if you somehow pass all 3, you still would have to take an elective, which could take 2-3 months to pass." I told him, "I'll take them today." The tests were Math (my favorite), English (my least favorite) and Science (something I kinda liked). I went into their computer room, super quiet, I was all alone and for the next 3-4 hours, I took the 3 tests. I told the person in charge I was done and I waited for about 5 minutes for the results. My heart was pounding, hoping that I had passed. By the grace of God, the lady tells me, I got all 15 credits. I passed all 3! I took the paper with the results to the counselor. He is surprised and congratulates me.

But I still needed 5 credits. He told me I had to take an elective class. I chose Art History. He still persisted that it was impossible to complete this within 1 month. Those classes normally take 3 months to complete, but I told him I'd try anyway.

When I got to class, I was given a textbook. They told me, "Read this and when you are ready for the chapter test, I'll take the textbook and hand you the test." At the end of the week, I take the chapter 1 test, pass. I had like 20 more to go. I asked the teacher how often I could take the test, and they responded, "You could take the test everyday if you wanted to, but that's up to you."

So I did just that. This is when I first experienced the small "5 Hour Energy" drink. I went to the gas station, saw this little bottle and thought, "If this can give me the kick I need, it could help me." Oh man did it wake me up. My eyelids were stuck open. I knocked out 1 to 2 chapters A DAY. I completed my entire book in the next 3 weeks.

When I showed my counselor I was done at the end of the month, he was so surprised that I was able to do this. He gave me my certificate, I called my recruiter and told him the good news. I was leaving for Boot Camp in about 10 days. I would end up serving in the Elite Military Branch, the United States Marine Corps for the next 7 ½ years. God helped me get to this point and I thank Him with all of my heart.

My Time in the Corps

During this time, God trained me to be a better, more disciplined leader. He showed me my true work ethic, enhanced my leadership skills, and how I would react to injustice and unfairness. Moving me from unit to unit, leading small groups to Platoon Sergeant of 50 Marines. I learned how to take care of my team, mentor them, look out for their welfare and encourage them to reach their full potential as Marines and reach their goals in life.

While I served, I also battled with anger, lust addiction, and mental breakdowns. Another story for another time. But all these things God helped me resolve and He has delivered me. I met some horrible people but I also met the greatest people I still talk to today. I thank God for my military experience, as well as the battles I faced. It has made me stronger and it has also made me realize how much I needed Him.

I will never regret my time in the service. I would do it all over again. Of course I'd make a few changes to how I conducted myself but I'd choose the same MOS, same units, same people, same struggles to build me up to who I am today.

In 2013, I married my best friend Delila, and we planned on buying a house as soon as possible. We had our daughter, our son, and she was pregnant by the time I would end my last enlistment in 2016. Because I moved so much, as a child and as an adult, I made it my mission to never rent if I didn't have to. I will not have my kids go through what I went through. I will buy a house one day and do all that I can to minimize moving from place to place.

Our First House Testimony

At the end of 2016, I was honorably discharged from the Marine Corps and began my life as a veteran in the civilian world. With no time to waste, around Jan-Feb 2017, we applied for a home loan. Here is where the journey begins with how God redirected our paths and refocused our goals. At that time, our minds were set on all the best things; big home, big backyard, best area, best schools, and everything anyone could hope for in a home.

We got approved! But we were disappointed to find out that we qualified for a price range that only allowed us to purchase a tiny home in the worst areas of our county. We tried to figure out how we could increase the loan amount by negotiating with the loan officer what we could do, but it was what it was.

Delila and I talked about it and decided, maybe this is what God wants. This really humbled us to trust God and pray that wherever we buy, He would protect us and guide us. So we said to ourselves, "Ok, looks like we're going to buy a home in a bad area because that's all we can afford. If this is what God wants, then we will trust Him."

Suddenly, I got a letter in the mail… it was the VA. They just approved my military disability compensation. Now any veteran would tell you, this is a quick response. It would take some veterans months before they got a response from the VA, and sometimes years.

This happened exactly in the middle of our home search. If I would have had this new income 2 weeks prior, and we would have tried buying a more expensive home than what God wanted us to buy. 2 weeks later, and we would have been in escrow for a tiny home in a bad area. God came through in His perfect timing.

We understood what God wanted us to do. We decided to budget ourselves, where if both of us could only work at minimum wage paying jobs, we would still be able to afford it. That's how we capped ourselves off and soon after, God blessed us with a home. And I'll tell you, it was the best one we saw within our budget. Thank You Father!

The first 2 years living in the home wasn't very pleasant. I remember someone getting shot 2 houses down during a party, homeless people living across the street; at times banging on my door while drugged out, and falling asleep on my porch chair. But I never regretted moving in, I was grateful for being able to have a home to call my own.

Why I Got My Realtor License

During the next 3 years, I learned a little about rental properties and got my Realtor license. Half the reason why, I wanted to invest in rental properties. The other half was because I wanted to help others achieve homeownership.

My parents were never able to buy a home, and I knew what it felt like to move and not be stable. If I'm able to help someone else through the process and answer the questions my parents had, I will. I want to genuinely help and advise them to achieve their goal which seems so impossible for some. And that's not true! With this license, I was able to help my Mom finally purchase a house. This was such a blessing. From the fact that I got my license partially because my parents weren't able to buy a home, to helping my Mom buy her first house, is incredible.

Before I get into my second house testimony, I'd like to share all that God taught me and how He has grown my character. Most of which I believe I needed to learn, before God gave me this great responsibility. If you're just eager to read the dream house testimony, it's a longer story, just go to Chapter 5 now. Then come back to Chapter 3: Life Lessons.

CHAPTER 3

Life Lessons

Only 50 cents!

I GOT TO A POINT IN MY CAREER WHERE I FELT LIKE I WAS DOING more than I was expected to do and I wasn't getting paid accordingly. I read in a business book to ask for a raise once in a while. First to prove your worth and give maximum value as an asset then go in for an ask. So I did just that. I worked hard, took initiative to do more tasks beyond my job responsibilities, then I wrote up an email of how much I was doing and politely asked to be considered for a raise. I had great evidence to back up my claims. I sent it and got a response a few weeks later.

Manager: "Here is the raise you asked for Christian."
Me: "50 cents? That's all they approved? May I ask how much you asked for on my behalf?"
Manager: "50 cents."
Me: "...ok. Thank you."

I was so angry. I was getting underpaid and after all my work and justifications, my manager only put in a request for 50 cents. I felt so unwanted and under appreciated. I thought, "These people don't value me. Is that all I'm worth to them?" Now for you who think I should have been grateful and 50 cents is something. I have to say, you're right, I was being ungrateful.

After I cooled off and spoke to my Father-in-law, I prayed about it. "God, I understand You're ultimately my boss. I shouldn't have to ask for a raise. I need to work hard as though I work unto You and You will give me increase if that's Your will. I won't care about my pay anymore. In this, I will trust You Lord."

9 months later I received a $1.50 raise, 6 months later $2, 6 Months another $2, 3 Months another $2, 3 Months later $1, 3 Months later another $1, and the rest I won't bore you with. God is taking care of everything. He keeps His promises. You seek Him and He will take care of everything else for your family and all of your needs. I now only expect God to bless me. I won't conform to what the world teaches, but it should be normal for a believer to see blessings come from our Father. He is a good Father. Commit your work to Him and you will see success or a shift to a better direction.

Stop Complaining

I started to complain a lot. I would tell everyone my problems and how I'm trying my best to trust God through it all. I asked God to help me with my complaining. One day He told me, "Stop complaining out of your mouth." Did God just tell me to shut my mouth? God is my Father, He lovingly told me to stop complaining but to get the point across, He was basically telling me to shut my mouth about these things. And I did just as He said, I stopped speaking negative speech over my life and expressing no gratitude for what I did have.

There is a Proverb saying the foolish vent out their feelings but a wise person holds their tongue. So this made sense. And another says a foolish person seems wise when they keep quiet.

"A fool vents all his feelings, But a wise man holds them back."
Proverbs 29:11 NKJV

"Even fools are thought wise if they keep silent, and discerning if they hold their tongues."
Proverbs 17:28 NIV

So as I obeyed, my heart would be at peace for a couple of weeks. But then I began to feel like complaining again, but I didn't allow it to come out in my words. But I knew it was in my heart. I was basically complaining in my mind. I went to God again and said, "Lord I'm not complaining with my words like You said, but I still feel it in my heart. Can you please remove it from me?"

He responded, "Because you have been obedient in what I told you with your words, I will take what is in your heart." And He took it away! I feel like He was saying, it's my job to control what I say, but He takes care of the heart and spiritual side when we go to Him. I'm telling you, I had no thoughts of negativity in my life. I was only grateful, my mind was calm and clear. It was incredible. I did what I had to do without complaining. I felt complete contentment. I finally felt complete peace and joy.

When trials came, I just focused on what God was teaching me in those moments. I treated every "negative" experience into a teaching lesson from my Father. I didn't reject it but embraced it. If someone or something was against me, I knew it would only make me stronger. I got to the point where I asked for growth and at times, opposition would come and I would get excited, not for the pain I would have to endure, but for the outcome.

A year passed, and I began to have these complaining feelings in my heart again. Of course I turned to God and asked for help controlling my tongue. Then the thoughts began to come. I asked God to take it away as He did before. He said, "No."

I was surprised. I was like, "What do You mean Lord? I'm obedient just as before with controlling my tongue. Last time, You took what was in my heart. Why aren't You going to do it again? I thought this was the part where we relied on You."

"You're wrong." He answered. "You were a weaker person then. So I helped you. I can't spoon feed you forever. Now I need you to grow and feed yourself. It's time for you to control what's in your heart." Then this scripture came to mind.

"...bringing every thought into captivity to the obedience of Christ,"
2 Corinthians 10:5 NKJV

God wants us to captivate our thoughts, He doesn't do it for us. He is able to help us, just as He helped me before, but He wants us to grow up and learn to control our words AND our thoughts. Today I'm still learning how to do this, as it's very difficult. I believe the more we read the Word, the more our spirit is fed. Being disciplined to read our word, abide in Christ, and truly seeking the Kingdom will allow us to conquer our flesh. In turn, giving our spirit a fighting chance.

Is complaining really that bad? Yes. Check out these verses.

"Now when the people complained, it displeased the Lord; for the Lord heard it, and His anger was aroused. So the fire of the Lord burned among them, and consumed some in the outskirts of the camp."
Numbers 11:1 NKJV

"And the Lord spoke to Moses and Aaron, saying, "How long shall I bear with this evil congregation who complain against Me? I have heard the complaints which the children of Israel make against Me. Say to them, 'As I live,' says the Lord, 'just as you have spoken in My hearing, so I will do to you: The carcasses of you who have complained against Me shall fall in this wilderness..."
Numbers 14:26-29 NKJV

"nor <u>complain</u>, as some of them also <u>complained</u>, and were destroyed by the destroyer."
1 Corinthians 10:10 NKJV

"..."Behold, the Lord comes with ten thousands of His saints, to execute judgment on all, to convict all who are ungodly among them of all their ungodly deeds which they have committed in an ungodly way, and of all the harsh things which ungodly sinners have spoken against Him." These are <u>grumblers</u>, <u>complainers</u>, walking according to their own lusts; and they mouth great swelling words, flattering people to gain advantage."
Jude 1:14-16 NKJV

Now when we read these, we are talking about those who complain against God. If you are struggling and need to vent and talk about something, go to God. It's ok to talk about something that is bothering you but it's another thing to complain to God about what He is doing in your life. Just as David said it in his psalm.

"I pour out my complaint before Him; I declare before Him my trouble."
Psalm 142:2 NKJV

I also believe talking to your spouse about something that is bothering you is completely ok and together, as one. You will resolve it or at least pray together about something that is difficult at that point in your life. If you aren't married and want to talk to someone, again it's ok to talk to a friend about something that is bothering you. Just beware when you speak ill about God and complain AGAINST Him. Stop, examine yourself first, and then be open to constructive criticism. I'm sure the person you are complaining to, you have some level of trust towards. Maybe they have a decent handle on what you're going through or they have already overcome it. Now if they are in the same boat, be careful not to just be pulled in deeper and complain even more. Find someone who is willing to help you get into a better place.

Always go to God about everything. Good and bad. He will hear your heart and give you peace. If you're just walking around telling everyone that everything is horrible, people will label you as a complainer and won't want to hear it. Better yet, you'll attract other complainers. Then before you know it, you're enlisted in the company's complaining group, and all you ever talk about is how much life is terrible and whose life is worse. You will begin to feel worse and possibly get worse as you are verbally agreeing with curses over your so-called "horrible life". Remove yourself from this group. Get around someone who speaks life and hope, rather than depression and anger. Renounce all the negative words you have spoken over your life, over your children's lives, and ask God to help you.

God I'm Worried

We all know from the Bible, Jesus tells us there is no point in worrying. As it doesn't add an hour to our lives and to trust God and He will provide what we need.

"Therefore I tell you, <u>do not worry</u> about your life, what you will eat or drink; or about your body, what you will wear. Is not life more than food, and the body more than clothes? Look at the birds of the air; they do not sow or reap or store away in barns, and yet your heavenly Father feeds them. Are you not much more valuable than they? Can any one of you by <u>worrying</u> add a single hour to your life?"
Matthew 6:25-27 NIV

"Who of you by <u>worrying</u> can add a single hour to your life? Since you cannot do this very little thing, why do you <u>worry</u> about the rest?"
Luke 12:25-26 NIV

I did the same thing as I did with complaining; I would say I'm worried about something. God would tell me not to speak this. I wouldn't speak of it, but I still felt it. God would remove the feelings in my heart. Then a few months would pass and God would teach me how to control my emotions and to trust in Him through worrisome situations. Over time, it got easier not to worry, I just trusted God in everything. Something comes up that is unknown and has a possibility of going wrong, I would get the feeling and thought to worry about it, I'd capture it, then throw it away. No overwhelming thoughts of my future. No matter what happened to me, I would simply brush it off and trust God.

Do not worry or be anxious, but rather be thankful and pray. Then God's peace will guard your heart and mind through Jesus Christ.

"Be anxious for nothing, but in everything by prayer and supplication, with thanksgiving, let your requests be made known to God; and the peace of God, which surpasses all understanding, will guard your hearts and minds through Christ Jesus."
Philippians 4:6-7 NKJV

Where does worry come from? Fear. Understand, worry is fear of the unknown. It's a state of anxiety and uncertainty. But obviously not just anything unknown or uncertain, it's fear of something going wrong. In this, I'd say, let it go. If you are worried about something or someone and have no control over it, give it to God and watch Him work. Don't pray saying God I trust You and I will no longer worry about it, then seconds after you say "Amen", you begin to worry. You are doubting God, you may be canceling the prayer you just spoke. Pray and TRUST. Let it go. Thank God for what will come afterward. It's very difficult to do this, but it's where we need to get to. At points like this, you may need to fast, to humble yourself, gain some self-control and rely completely on God. Press into Him and He will give you rest. Come to Jesus and you will find rest.

Don't worry and don't have an anxious mind but seek God and His righteousness, then He will take care of you. So…

"Humble yourselves, therefore, under God's mighty hand, that He may lift you up in due time. Cast all your anxiety on Him because He cares for you."
1 Peter 5:6-7 NIV

"Then Jesus said, "Come to me, all of you who are weary and carry heavy burdens, and I will give you rest. Take my yoke upon you. Let me teach you, because I am humble and gentle at heart, and you will find rest for your souls. For my yoke is easy to bear, and the burden I give you is light."
Matthew 11:28-30 NLT

"And do not seek what you should eat or what you should drink, nor have an anxious mind. For all these things the nations of the world seek after, and your Father knows that you need these things."
Luke 12:29-30 NKJV

"But seek first the kingdom of God and His righteousness, and all these things shall be added to you. Therefore do not worry about tomorrow, for tomorrow will worry about its own things. Sufficient for the day is its own trouble."
Matthew 6:33-34 NKJV

To summarize, I captivated my thoughts on worry and God gave me peace. It got to the point where I didn't care what happened around me, I would just be at peace and give it to God. Pray today for freedom from these overwhelming thoughts. Pray for God to help you quiet the voices of defeat and fear of the unknown. Invite His Spirit in.

"For <u>God has not given us a spirit of fear</u>, but of power, of love, and <u>of a sound mind</u>."
2 Timothy 1:7 NKJV

A Future Solar Testimony

Latest test of my faith and ability to handle worry. At the end of 2022, we just had our solar panels installed. Finally up and running but many small problems we were facing with communication with the solar company. We had questions about the Mechanic Lien against our house, the contractors who installed them never returned to replace broken roof tiles or paint the pipes along the house. But the solar company never responded, I was getting very impatient, even telling them they have the worst customer service I have ever experienced.

At the beginning of 2023, our solar company went out of business. My heart naturally dropped into worry. "What is going to happen? What are we going to do? Who do we go to if a solar panel is broken? Are the contractors even paid? Will we have to pay them out of pocket? We now don't have a warranty on repairs, what do we do?" A moment of worry passed, I allowed these thoughts to come, then I pushed them away. Then I started to think, it happens. These sorts of things happen to many people. Problem arises, but what am I going to do about it? Cry? No. How am I going to handle it? I'm going to figure it out. I didn't cause this. It was out of my control. I did my research as well as many others. Then I started to think.

I prayed about this. I remember in 2021, I asked God what I should do financially. He is my King and my God. I go to Him for future projects and financial advice as any other servant of God. I felt solar was a great option to consider. I did research and picked the best option in our area at the time. I prayed that if this wasn't the right company, that God would let me know and I'll go elsewhere, or for Him to make something go wrong in the transaction. I got a green light all the way through, to the point of installation, city approval and working just fine.

Fast forward to 2023. As I thought these things, I smiled and knew God is up to something. Something great is going to happen and it will be for our good and it will bring Him glory. He is the God of the universe, why should I worry? Maybe the bankruptcy will pay off our loan completely. That would be awesome, wouldn't it? I don't know but my faith isn't wavering. I always expect God to move in extraordinary ways knowing what He is capable of. I can't wait to see what happens next because God ALWAYS comes through. I will update you all on social media, once I find out what it is. Another great testimony to come. All glory to God.

Why do I feel this way? How can I be sure God will direct my path? Even though I made plans, why do I think God's ultimate purpose will prevail? Why do I think all things will work together for our good?

"You can make many plans, but the Lord's purpose will prevail."
Proverbs 19:21 NLT

"And we know that all things work together for good to those who love God, to those who are the called according to His purpose."
Romans 8:28 NKJV

"Trust in the Lord with all your heart, And lean not on your own understanding; In all your ways acknowledge Him, And He shall direct your paths."
Proverbs 3:5-6 NKJV

"A man's heart plans his way, But the Lord directs his steps."
Proverbs 16:9 NKJV

I love these verses. We can create the best plan, or many plans, but the Lord will direct our steps. And notice, He isn't forcing us to take action, WE are the ones stepping forward, trusting Him. And once we take that step, before it hits the ground, God will shift where it should be placed so it's according to His plan and will. Because we are trusting Him and not leaning on our own understanding. Because we are acknowledging Him in all our ways. He will not allow us to utterly fall. He is the best Father.

If your child created a plan then looked at you and said, "I'm walking this way because I believe it's what you want. I love you and I trust you." Then they blindly step out. As a loving parent, aren't you going to move their foot to step somewhere safely and in the correct direction? God sees the future and knows how each step will affect our character and our path. He sees our heart and our true motive and intentions. He is the true living God. He knows what's best. He loves us much more than we will ever imagine.

If you do face a trial, and are continuously trusting Him, then know that it's part of His greater plan. If you ever feel God is disciplining you, He may be setting you straight for your good, because He loves you. Delight in His actions.

"because the <u>LORD disciplines those he loves</u>, as a father the son he delights in."
Proverbs 3:12 NIV

"For the <u>LORD disciplines those he loves</u>, and he punishes each one he accepts as his child."
Hebrews 12:6 NLT

"Yea, though I walk through the valley of the shadow of death, I will fear no evil; For You are with me; <u>Your rod and Your staff, they comfort me</u>."
Psalms 23:4 NKJV

His rod was used to discipline and correct us; as well as ward off the enemies. His staff is used to guide us and pull us in close to Him; as well as pick us up when we stumble and fall into a pit, and

He'll never utterly cast us down. These were used by sheppards to lead and protect their sheep. So be comforted by His rod and staff if you are a child of God and are putting your complete trust in Him.

"The <u>steps of a good man are ordered by the Lord</u>, And He delights in his way. Though he fall, <u>he shall not be utterly cast down</u>; For the Lord upholds him with His hand."
Psalm 37:24 NKJV

"For I know the plans I have for you," says the Lord. <u>"They are plans for good and not for disaster, to give you a future and a hope."</u>
Jeremiah 29:11 NLT

Stop Being Self-Righteous

There was a point where I tried being what the Bible said to be. Be kind, love one another, be slow to anger, love God with all your heart, seek the Kingdom and His righteousness, repent from sin, be patient, be generous, forgive others, and so on. I found it so difficult to do these things, the more I tried to do these things, I got tired. I began to ask God how any of us could do these things successfully. I read:

"And do not be conformed to this world, but be <u>transformed</u> by the <u>renewing of your mind</u>, that you may prove what is that good and acceptable and perfect will of God."
Romans 12:2 NKJV

Be transformed by the renewing of your mind? Am I supposed to renew my mind? How do I do this?

"Set your mind on things above, not on things on the earth."
Colossians 3:2 NKJV

Set our minds on things above? So I'm supposed to set my mind on God? And when I thought about this, I came to a revelation. I won't try to do these things, but abide in God and He will transform me, He will renew my mind and my heart. In other words, I won't force myself to be kind, but let God change my character. This brought me to a place of relief. No more do I have to try and be a good person, I will BE a good person because God has changed me inside. And is constantly changing us to be good, kind, loving, honorable, generous, just, honest, loyal, merciful, and righteous people. Not because of us, but because of Him and for His glory. This is why the word says to look at the fruit of people. If they are one moment kind and patient, but live a lifestyle of cruelty, lying, thieving, sin and evil, we know they don't have the fruit of the Holy Spirit and aren't transformed. We are to be watchful, keeping an eye out for wolves in sheep's clothing. God looks at the heart of man, we see the outer appearance and how people act. We need to always test the spirits according to God's word and teachings.

I say all this because I tried hard but I got tired of being "nice" or "kind". When I got grumpy or completely out of patience, my default character would kick in. I was my true self. I found myself upset, not kind, not as merciful as I thought I was and not as loving. But once I finally understood that I don't have to force myself to be kind but to let God change me. I was naturally kind. I didn't have to try anymore. I became a kind person. I'm not self-righteous anymore. I remember thinking I was holier than thou, that I was better than others who weren't as kind as the bible said we should be. But this is evil and dangerous. We can become prideful and think I'm kind because of me, I'm righteous because of me. And not because of Jesus Christ. We are righteous because of God, because of Jesus. He clothes me with this righteousness. We seek His righteousness. I am in right standing with God because of my belief and faith in Him and in His precious Son. His Holy Spirit will guide me, speak to me, and train me.

Fruit of the Holy Spirit

For the longest time I didn't understand what the fruits of the Holy Spirit were. Then when I did understand, I still had to figure out how I was supposed to grow them in my life. Here are the fruits:

- Love
- Joy
- Peace
- Longsuffering/Forbearance/Patience
- Kindness
- Goodness
- Faithfulness
- Gentleness
- Self-Control

"22 But the fruit of the Spirit is love, joy, peace, longsuffering, kindness, goodness, faithfulness, 23 gentleness, self-control. Against such there is no law."
Galatians 5:22-23 NKJV

What do you mean "fruit"? When you read *Galatians 5:19-21 NKJV,*

"19 Now the <u>works of the flesh</u> are evident, which are: adultery, fornication, uncleanness, lewdness, 20 idolatry, sorcery, hatred, contentions, jealousies, outbursts of wrath, selfish ambitions, dissensions, heresies, 21 envy, murders, drunkenness, revelries, and the like; of which I tell you beforehand, just as I also told you in time past, that those who practice such things will not inherit the kingdom of God."

It talks about the "works of the flesh", the evil desires of the flesh. Then when it goes on to verse 22, it mentions "fruit", "But the fruit of the Spirit...", as you can see above, it takes a turn to what is holy. So I believe it can also be said that the "works of the

Spirit" are love, joy, peace, and so on. And the same for the "fruit" of the flesh is "adultery, fornication, uncleanness, lewdness, idolatry, sorcery, hatred, contentions, jealousies, outbursts of wrath, selfish ambitions, dissensions, heresies, envy, murders, drunkenness" and so on mentioned through verses 19-21.

Now that we understand that it's more of an outward act of our desires and not just feelings. With all this being said, we're not ONLY to be internally loving, joyful, peaceful, patient, kind, good, faithful, gentle and have self-control BUT to act these things outwardly. We are to act in love for others. Even through hardships, to be joyful knowing that God will take care of us and is always in control. Then show others how to be joyful in the Lord through any circumstance, as hard as this may be. We are to be patient with others and look past their mistakes and flaws. But to look at them with love of God, through God's perspective. And not act upon any emotions alone. We are kind to others especially when they don't deserve it. Go out of our way to be kind, NOT because God said so, but because your spirit is transformed and you ARE a kind person. Its no longer an act you have to force, it's automatic. And over time it gets easier as this fruit grows. Understand?

We are to be gentle, not rough around the edges. God gave us faces that reveal our emotional state, health state, and even our spiritual state. Our countenance shows if we are sad, upset, angry, happy, joyful, worried, healthy, sick, and so on. We can gentle with someone we can perceive as upset, and ask what is wrong? Just as God asks Cain, why his countenance has fallen in Genesis 4:6. We can see how our words affect someone else and quickly recognize where something we said could have changed how they feel. There are many books that try and help us grow as people in society and watching body language, face expressions and live at peace. But if God never gave us this, it would be very difficult to understand how people feel without words. Most people don't pour out their hearts openly, they show it on their face and someone asks if they are ok or can see that they are happy and invite others to smile.

We are to have self-control. This includes controlling our temperament. Starting as a child, most of us are taught not to throw tantrums. Well, as adults, we are always learning to watch our words, our behavior and our actions. Why? To live at peace of course. Self-control is huge. Its the first trait we need help with, it will also help us start our journey with God. When God says we shouldn't gossip, murder, lie, lust, envy, and so on. Its very difficult because its part of every human heart, our natural human flesh, our sinful desire. But we are to control it. Every sin starts with a thought, a temptation, by our own desires. That's where the enemy starts. They don't force us to sin, they tempt us. And if you don't have self-control, we act upon it. We choose to sin, nobody forces you. The enemy never has power you haven't given it. We must resist. We are to control ourselves when desires come. Without submission to God, most desires will come from our flesh and the enemy. No temptation is from God.

"Let no one say when he is tempted, "I am tempted by God"; for <u>God cannot be tempted by evil, nor does He Himself tempt anyone</u>. But <u>each one is tempted when he is drawn away by his own desires and enticed</u>. Then, when <u>desire has conceived</u>, it gives birth to sin; and sin, when it is full-grown, brings forth death."
James 1:13-15 NKJV

If you fall into sin, confess it to God, repent and be forgiven in Jesus name. Now let's go into how we should recognize others based on THEIR fruit. We can look at what Jesus says in Matthew 7.

"15 "Beware of false prophets, who come to you in sheep's clothing, but inwardly they are ravenous wolves. 16 <u>You will know them by their fruits</u>. Do men gather grapes from thornbushes or figs from thistles? 17 Even so, every good tree bears good fruit, but a bad tree bears bad fruit. 18 A good tree cannot bear bad fruit, nor can a bad tree bear good fruit.

19 Every tree that does not bear good fruit is cut down and thrown into the fire. 20 Therefore <u>by their fruits you will know them</u>."
Matthew 7:15-20 NKJV

So we can know someone by the fruit they bear. In other words, we can know who someone truly is, by what they do and act. But what about this scripture? Isn't it mentioning wolves in sheep's clothing, aren't these wolves pretending to have good fruit. I think it goes deeper. They may pretend in public or social media, but when the scripture says a bad tree can't bear good fruit, you look at them long enough and the fruit will show. You get close enough and you'll begin to smell the rotten fruit they truly have. Not what was perceived from afar but really getting to know them and how they think. Test the spirits by what you learn from God, from His scriptures, and the Holy Spirit. Listen closely and use your discernment.

And the same in reverse, someone with a good tree will bear good fruit. You will see love, joy, peace, gentleness, self-control in their character and not hatred, envy, murder and the sort. You will notice some people will identify themselves as angry, lustful, or homosexual. They say "It's who I am. Without it, who am I? I wouldn't know how to function."

Now the question may come up, how do I become a good tree? Well I believe that's being rooted in Jesus Christ. The worldly people will try to be "good" but they are spiritually dead. They will never feel true love and peace. Only the temporary counterfeits the devil has given them. When someone is a branch of the living tree of God, they will begin to bear good fruit and God will prune the bad fruit you once held. Sometimes it hurts, but it's for your own good. The more we abide in Jesus Christ, the more He abides in us.

God will work on 1 fruit at a time. I noticed when I would face trials, God was growing the fruit of love or patience. Once I accomplished growth to a certain level, He would move me onto another fruit, until every fruit has grown to a certain point. Then

He would make His round again through each fruit reaching higher levels and deeper into my heart. All this while He is pruning my bad fruit. If I fight against Him and feed into those bad habits, I'm depriving the good fruit.

Don't try to force yourself to do what the fruit says, but be in Christ and the fruit will describe who you are, not just a list of things you should be. For example, like I said before, I've tried to do all these things but it got exhausting. When I got tired and ran out of energy, I would default back to who I really am in my heart. The true fruit would show. I resulted in becoming angry, bitter, and rude. But in my mind, I was deceived. I thought I was good because I was doing all that the fruit were saying to be. God told me I was being self-righteous. So I gave up on trying to do these things and just focused on Him. This was a shift in my life. When opportunities would arise, I didn't have to "try" anything, it just was. I was already in my relaxed state. Almost like I truly found spiritual peace and I defaulted in being gentle, loving, joyful, patient, and much more.

Here is where the enemy comes in. The devil and his minions would now try to get you out of this peaceful state and tempt you to turn back to your evil reactions. But here is where we need to become spiritual aware, having discernment, captivating every thought and bringing it to the obedience of Jesus Christ. Testing the spirits, countering the enemy's attacks with the sword of the Spirit, which is the Word of God. The enemy knows which buttons to push and when to do it. Be ready, be watchful children of God.

God I Will Show You I Love You

I got to a place where I wanted to help people, to show God that I loved Him. Heal those that need healing. Conduct deliverances and free people of demons. All to show God I loved Him. But what I learned was I didn't need to do these things to be a better believer or follower of Jesus Christ. I need to spend time with Him. I need my heart to be His.

I once heard that it's like a wife telling her husband that she loves him so much, she wants to give him kids, but never spends time with him, she is never intimate with him. Same thing with God. How are we supposed to grow a relationship with Him if we never spend time with Him? We leave the house and love other people but don't go to the quiet place. We think doing God's will is loving Him. But that's wrong. I felt like God was telling me, "If you want to show Me you love Me, then love Me by spending time with Me."

How many of us are doing this? Ok God, I'm going to fast, pray for others, serve at the church, join a ministry, start a ministry, lead a church, donate to others, pay my tithes, and many other things we think we are doing to show God we love Him. But most of us get burnt out, especially those who thought God owed them something. Those who think God needs to make all their problems go away. The truth is, we need to glorify Him, praise Him, honor Him, thank Him in all things, expecting NOTHING in return. Something goes wrong, we praise Him and say, "Your will be done my God. You are all powerful, full of grace and mercy. You do as You wish. I worship You. I love You. Thank You, King of the Universe." Then trust Him through it all. Look up and know that He is God.

Purple Robe

One time I was leaving work, and I looked up. The sun was behind the few clouds in the sky. But nevertheless, it seemed majestic. Suddenly I felt like I was transformed. Like I was in different clothing and shined a bit. I was wearing a King's purple robe. My long purple robe along with my gold sash, I felt like royalty to the highest. "Why am I feeling like this?" I thought.

God was showing me how HE sees me. I began to view myself as a child of the Most High God, being a king in spirit but a servant on this earth. Then I found myself wearing servant's clothes, feeding the poor and loving people like if I was an undercover king in his kingdom, watching out for his people. And I believe that's what God was showing me. He views His children like Kings and Queens with all of our perfections He created us to be. We are His masterpiece. And He sends us out to help those in need and to love one another. Not being prideful in Christ but humble. Knowing who we are in Him and using this confidence and faith to reach everyone.

If only we viewed ourselves this way everyday, there wouldn't be a need to try and obtain fame, money, and sources of temporary satisfaction. We should be viewing other believers in the faith with this same love and respect. Imagine jumping on a Zoom call with other believers and we all were wearing royalty attire, discussing how to reach the lost.

Then I imagined all of us, walking together towards God's throne. Left and right there are stadiums facing this road we are on, filled with angels blastings their horns and trumpets, as we arrived and walked. God was huge, sitting on His throne. And all of us were wearing our royalty clothing. Just seemed so incredible. It was heaven for sure. We did our duty on earth and now we were gathering to our heavenly Father.

My wife sent me a message right in the middle of me writing this. She didn't know I was writing about these royalty robes. Here is the passage she sent me.

"1 Then he showed me Joshua the high priest standing before the Angel of the Lord, and Satan standing at his right hand to oppose him. 2 And the Lord said to Satan, "The Lord rebuke you, Satan! The Lord who has chosen Jerusalem rebuke you! Is this not a brand plucked from the fire?" 3 Now Joshua was clothed with filthy garments, and was standing before the Angel. 4 Then He answered and spoke to those who stood before Him, saying, "Take away the filthy garments from him." And to him He said, "See, I have removed your iniquity from you, and I will clothe you with rich robes." 5 And I said, "Let them put a clean turban

on his head." So they put a clean turban on his head, and they put the
clothes on him. And the Angel of the Lord stood by."
Zechariah 3:1-5 NKJV

In verse 4, we see God saying "See, I have removed your iniquity
(the filthy garments), and I will clothe you with <u>rich robes</u>." My wife
immediately remembered when I told her this vision I had of royalty
clothes. We were both amazed at how God works like this. So this
explains why God sees us this way. He clothed us. He removed our
iniquity. Next time you are struggling in this world, if you are a child
of God, look into the sky and remember how God sees you and how
He has clothed you.

*"But as many as received Him, to them He gave the right to become
<u>children of God</u>, to those who believe in His name"*
John 1:12 NKJV

Javier says "God I Quit"

At work I get this opportunity to train in Texas. I had never been
there before and when I looked at the area, my good friend from
the Marine Corps lived nearby. I thought, "This would be a great
opportunity to hang out with him." But in my heart I also felt this
wasn't a coincidence, I was being sent. Sent to speak to Javier on a
matter I knew little about.

When I told him I was going to be there, he was excited just as
much as I was. He achieved his degree in Mechanical Engineering in
a prestigious college there. He got an amazing GPA. He had a house
being built for him. He had a decent job. So it seems everything was
going alright for him. But we discussed our paths in life and our
passion to do more, we felt like we plateaued. We both had similar
feelings about our jobs. Thinking there has to be more to life than
these career paths we were on. When we talk about God, he tells me

he believes but I felt he wasn't fully committed. But I was the same way a few years before.

When I showed up to Texas and met him the first night, I automatically wanted to catch up more than usual. He tells me about his relationship and why he felt stuck at his current job. I can completely relate. I felt the exact way, but I told him that we needed to trust God and His timing. He continues to tell me how he has done everything he could to move forward but still feel held back. Trying to find that career where he could manage operations.

We both love helping people. When in the Marine Corps, we used to mentor and counsel our Marines to better themselves and achieve more. But we were both in jobs where we couldn't do this. He is in charge of accounts, not people he could pour into. And I'm in charge of repairing a machine, not people I could pour into. We both can excel in really watching out for our team, putting ourselves on the line for our subordinates to success. We did everything we could for them. But not having this option today, is awful. It feels like everything we accomplished in growing our character as leaders is almost wasted. I have these questions, "Why God? Why have you shown me what I can do, building me up, just to be working at a place where it's not needed? Why build me up to be a good leader who actually cares about people, but not put me in a position where I can help others? My heart aches to do MORE but I'm stuck in a place where I feel not wanted. Please God change my path. Change my career for that I can feel fulfilled in helping others."

Javier felt this way as well. I told him of what happened in my marriage and other times in my life that I needed to let go and allow God to take over. He said, "I don't know why I am where I am. I thought I'd be further by now. I'm doing everything I can." And I said, "So quit. Maybe it's time to stop. You tried everything you could. Now let God take over." Then it clicked, he said, "That's it! I realize everything I have done was because God has helped me but now I need to quit. Quit doing it my way and allow Him to do what He wants. I have to let go." Later that night, we prayed and he said he felt like a weight lifted off of him. Peace came over him. During the next week we hung out before I left back home.

Almost a month after I returned home, he told me this incredible story. He was at work and his boss told him to take a longer lunch than usual. Then said, "You know what, take the rest of the day off." Javier was a bit surprised but was grateful that it happened and took off. That day there was also a veteran's event. He decided to go to it. He wasn't planning on going because he was going to be working all day. He sees someone who knows and enters a small chat about work. His friend remembers that Javier was looking for an operations type role and asks how the search was going. He explains why he was struggling to find the right fit and he would love to be an operations manager. Then suddenly the friend remembers, "My wife is actually looking for an operations manager." Turns around and tells his wife about Javier, they talk about the next job opportunity and set up an interview. A few days later, she interviews him and hires him. Javier told me he was so surprised. And they were going to pay him so well, he wouldn't need a pay raise for the rest of his life. THEN the bank calls him and tells him that they accidentally mixed up some numbers on his new house they were building and that they would pay his mortgage for the next 6 months.

He said, "God gave it to me on a silver platter. Everything went so smoothly so quickly. I know it was God." Then he proceeds to tell me how I need to trust God in whatever I do. I laugh because I was just telling him that a month ago and now he's preaching it. Thank you God for what You did in his life. I did tell him to be careful, because it may also get hard. The enemy will do everything he can make you think it should be easy from this point onward. But to fight, and not give up. It may get stressful but he has God's favor on him. Nothing can get in his way when God has assigned you there.

No Love = Damage

When we deliver a message to someone, how you deliver it matters. God tells us to love one another. This obviously applies to how you treat others, like lovingly delivering a correction. Some could say that "no love is no gain". Meaning if we don't deliver a message in love, then the person getting the message won't gain anything. They may not even accept the message because it came so bland and empty. So we should walk in love and really put our heart into giving the Good News to someone. Which I totally agree with. But I think of it a lot deeper.

If we don't show love, I believe we may be causing damage. It would be better not to deliver the message at all, if there isn't love behind it. Imagine someone coming to your door to give you the Great Message of God, that Jesus came and died for our sins but the person delivering it, is just condemning you. That you'll go to hell if you don't believe in Jesus and stop committing sins. Wouldn't you think, "This person woke up this morning, came to my door, just to tell me that I'm wrong and I should believe in this Jesus or I'm going to hell." ? Who is this person to tell me how I should live?

This is how most Christians give a bad taste in people's mouth about Jesus. Repent or go to hell. And we aren't even talking about the hypocrisy in the church. People will judge a religion based on its people. How they treat others and each other. How they uphold the "rules" they always talk about. When they see a believer who is always unhappy, complaining about life, talking like the world, walking like the world, while claiming to love God, and tell others to turn to Jesus; they will say, "See how your God doesn't do anything for you. You're not any happier than me and you claim to have this "Jesus". I'm good." Or worse, "You say all these things about love, peace, and joy but I see how you live and act, I don't even think you believe in what you say."

If you have experienced this, I want to say I'm sorry that other believers have misrepresented Jesus and the God of the Bible to you.

We are all sinners in need of a Savior and we all make mistakes, but this shouldn't be an excuse to live a life not according to how God wants us to live.

Now I believe not walking in love is actually damaging. If someone in the church ever offended you, you are going to know exactly what I'm saying. You can't try and correct someone without love, it's going to get really bad really fast. It's going to hurt more when it comes from a brother or sister in Christ. We are always supposed to be loving and respectful. We can rebuke with love. I'm not saying we always have to be "nice", we are called to be kind, love others, and to avoid strife (contensions with others). Always try to reconcile with those who have something against you. Whether it was your fault or not, try to reconcile. It doesn't mean you have to agree with everyone, but admit your wrongs and do your best to find a resolution. IF they still have something against you but you did everything you could with a clear and loving heart, I believe you can go to God with peace in heart, knowing you tried your best. Dust your feet off and go your way. Continue to seek God and His guidance, and if He ever wants you to try again, be open to it. Always listen to the Holy Spirit, He will convict you on what to do and what not to do.

"Therefore, if you are offering your gift at the altar and there remember that your brother or sister <u>has something against you</u>, leave your gift there in front of the altar. First <u>go and be reconciled to them</u>; then come and offer your gift."
Matthew 5:23-24 NIV

"It is to one's honor to <u>avoid strife</u>, but every fool is quick to quarrel.
Proverbs 20:3 NIV

"<u>Be kind and compassionate to one another</u>, forgiving each other, just as in Christ God forgave you."
Ephesians 4:32 NIV

You can kindly reject or rebuke someone. You can distance yourself from them if being around them is affecting your walk with God, or affecting your children in a negative way. But pray for them and love them from afar. And when you do come across them, don't avoid them; it's ok to talk to them and see how they are doing. Never hold a grudge or unforgiveness. This will block God's forgiveness from getting to you. And unforgiveness will open doors to demons and give them permission to affect your life.

"For if you forgive other people when they sin against you, your heavenly Father will also forgive you. But if you do not forgive others their sins, your Father will not forgive your sins."
Matthew 6:14-15 NIV

"Make allowance for each other's faults, and forgive anyone who offends you. Remember, the Lord forgave you, so you must forgive others."
Colossians 3:13 NLT

Relationships the Holy Way

We thrive to be kind and caring towards others. God teaches us to love our enemies and bless those who curse us. Jesus said,

"But I say to you, love your enemies, bless those who curse you, do good to those who hate you, and pray for those who spitefully use you and persecute you,"
Matthew 5:44 NKJV

When you read this, it's backwards of how most of us were taught. Maybe not from our parents but society. We see war, revenge, and justice being sentenced in court. This upside down Kingdom isn't popular, and to most comes off as weak. "Love your enemies"?! When you hear this, you may ask yourself, "I have to talk to them and hang out with them?" And that's understandable but it doesn't mean you do the things you do with the people you already love today. It's understanding they may be coming after you, but in your heart, you don't want harm for them, you forgive them, you can rebuke them and love them from afar. Praying for blessing on them and God to soften their hearts and help them. But nothing in you is against them, no matter what they have said, done, or going to do.

We aren't saying if someone is coming against your family physically and you have to just stand by and allow it to happen. Defend! Protect those who need it! May God give you strength to do so. We are saying that afterward, you forgive them and pray for those who acted upon evil intentions. You may hate the evil and evil actions, but not the person. There are evil influences all around us and that is what we are against. Hate sin as God hates sin. Love all who God loves, including Him.

Being Humble

A while back I learned not to exalt myself in ways of knowledge or material possession. I would listen to someone talk about this great deal they got, but once I found out it wasn't such a good deal, I would let them know. Their faces would change from excitement to disappointment. Not so much that they wished they knew what they got themselves into but rather wished I never said anything. I thought I was being helpful by letting them know the truth. I expected a thanks for the information. But they wanted me to be joyful and happy for them. So I began to be careful on what I say and how I say it, even if it is the truth.

For example, if someone told me they got a great deal on a car loan, and said they got 15% interest. I would cringe and want to say, "That's not a good interest rate. A good rate is around 2-3% on a used car and brand new you can get 0-2% depending on the term." From this they would be disappointed in themselves and most of the time, me. I learned to say, "Congratulations!" They don't want to hear how they just messed up. But at a later time, I would lovingly advise them on great banks and lenders who they could team up with, and make the deal even better! We do this because we care. If we didn't, we would just let them ride off into the sunset with a leech on their backs. We help each other by sharing knowledge and great tips in life to allow them to get ahead. We learn from each other's mistakes.

Same goes for having something better. Someone may approach you with this cool gadget or thing they just got, but if you know you have something better at home, don't say anything. They don't want to hear how yours is cooler, better, and got it at a bargain. Just be happy for them and congratulate them. Imagine every time you get something new and are excited to tell everyone, not to boast but in pure excitement, and each person you tell, only discourages you. Don't be that person. Be happy for them, share in the joy. Build that relationship, and later, guide them to make better and more wise decisions than you did. Eventually they will trust you, and because you weren't degrading or critical of their choices, they may come to you for advice on their next purchase or deal.

This really helped me understand how people think, act, react, and see what matters to them. Being humble also comes from not believing you're better than anyone else and being a know-it-all. Learning not to say, "I know.", "I know that.", and "I already know that." But having a learning and open mind. If you don't agree on some things, maybe you just don't understand it completely. Ask more questions. If you finally fully understand what is being said but simply don't agree with it, that's ok. Take the good, remove the bad, and place what is questionable in the back burner for a later research project. Don't just throw everything out. There may be truth to something you don't fully understand, maybe the Holy Spirit hasn't unlocked the understanding to it just yet. Now if it is bad, again the Holy Spirit will allow you to recognize it and rebuke it. Then teach others how you learned something was false advice, knowledge, teaching, or doctrine.

Forgiveness

The word says to forgive or we won't be forgiven. *"14 For if you forgive other people when they sin against you, your heavenly Father will also forgive you. 15 But if you do not forgive others their sins, your Father will not forgive your sins." Matthew 6:14-15 NIV.* So I make it my mission to forgive everyone for whatever they have done. I don't want those chains. I won't be held down by the enemy. I try to take a personal inventory of my relationships and who I'm talking about, how I talk about them, or how I feel about them, and so on. I like to say, "God I forgive everyone. I let it all go. I don't want to hold grudges or resentment. I rebuke all demons trying to enter by provoking me to get angry and be bitter and have wrath towards others."

At this point in my life, I felt pretty good about forgiving others quickly, swiftly, and not looking back. But... What happens when you're a Christian and for a good period of time haven't faced any prosecution, or anyone trying to wrong you, or come against you? Well, your guard will be down and something can slip through the cracks. It happened to me in mid 2022. I faced a moment where I held unforgiveness and wanted justice. I felt prideful, angry, wrathful, and wanted "righteous judgment" against this person. I wanted them to admit their wrong and correct the issue immediately and if they didn't, I prayed that they face intense hardship. Loss of job, business to shut down, allll the works. I wanted to tell them, "If you are being deceitful and don't admit to your wrong, you will reap what you sow and will face loss of clients and financial famine will hit their house." Wow. This was so immature and pitiful. But it was a simple misunderstanding and I took it too far. I wanted hardship for another human being. How cruel. It's ok to pursue justice legally and set things right, but not to make it a personal vendetta against them and wish harm physically, mentally or financially. We shall not have vengeance for it is God's. He will have the final say. So I let it all go. If this was a test I believe I failed. But after a couple of months, I renounced all I said in my heart, asked God for forgiveness and I let it go. I trust Him to take care of it all. This experience has humbled me and I'm grateful for this new sense of forgiveness awareness.

Again, it's ok to go after someone rightfully and legally, if they indeed caused an issue intentionally. If it was by accident, then the outcome looks promising. But that's it. Nothing more. If the verdict is in your favor, all glory to God. If it is not, all glory to God. It doesn't matter, you tried and that's it, don't make it personal! Pray for them, bless them, love them. If God says to let it go in the middle of a legal rightful pursuit, you better let it go, for the King has spoken. If you don't, I promise it will not look good for you. God may be trying to protect you from something or trying to teach you a lesson. You will soon find out.

Forgive and you will be forgiven. Don't let your prayers be hindered. Don't push away the favor that God has upon your life and your children's lives because someone hurt your feelings. Forgive your Father and Mother. Forgive your Step Dad and Step Mom. Forgive your wife or your husband. Forgive your ex-wife or your ex-husband. Forgive anyone who put you down. Forgive anyone who hurt someone you love. Forgiving them doesn't mean they deserve it, because you didn't when God sent His precious Son for you! Do you deserve forgiveness? Think about it. Do you deserve all the good that has happened to you? Put aside the bad for a moment and understand if you're reading or listening to this, YOU ARE ALIVE! You still have time to let it go. Remove those chains and walk away. This burden of unforgiveness. This distance from God you have been having. Throw those chains at His feet and say, "I'm done! These chains will no longer weigh me down. I forgive those who have wronged me and repent from all the anger I had against them. I'm sorry Lord that I took so long to be here. But I am here now because of Your magnificent grace and mercy. So I ask for Your forgiveness O God. I don't deserve it. I am a sinner in need of a Savior. Help me with my faith. Help me to forgive and continue to forgive because this battle isn't easy. In the name of the King of Kings and Lord of Lords, Jesus Christ, Amen.

Finally a Godly Husband & Father

I asked God to help me be a better Husband and Father. I found myself still struggling to help my wife with things around the house. I grew up with a Father who would sit on the couch after a long day at work, expecting my Mother to take care of the cleanliness and food in our house, even though she got out of work a couple of hours previously. So when I got married, I wanted to relax when I got home. But this isn't right.

To make this quick, I prayed and cried out to God to make me the husband and Father I'm supposed to be with His help. He began to show me by using management as an example. Why is it that I can be an amazing manager by watching out for my employees, co-workers, and leadership but neglect my spouse? I had more patience with people at work than I did with my wife and kids. I needed to step back and look at my family as if I were their manager, their leader. I look out for their needs and welfare. I held myself back at home because I didn't want to come off as weak if I served my wife a certain way or listened to what she said. Jesus was never looked at as weak when He washed His disciples' feet. So why do I feel I will be viewed as lesser? My wife is the weaker vessel, so I should be taking care of her just as God commanded me to. I should love her and show her I love her by my actions, not just by my words.

I started to learn how to listen to my wife as a leader, really separating my emotions and try to figure out how to help her. If I can listen to my team at work on how to do their job better and step in to help while knocking out my tasks as well, then how much more can I do that at home, for my family? So when I get home, I knock out my duties as the man of the house, then I focus on what more I can do for my house, my wife, and my kids. THEN I get to relax. AFTER everything that needs to get done, is done! I need to set an example for my children. To show them what being a Godly husband really looks like. To show them what being a Godly Dad looks like. I need to understand, I will never be the weaker vessel but I do need to step it up and lead my family in the way of God. I am the leader that God appointed me over this house and I will seek Him continually on how to do it, and through this I'm already in victory.

Thank You God for showing me all these things and lessons. There are many to come and I'll continue to share with others. You are my leader Jesus and I will follow. You are my Provider God, I will distribute what You bless me with. I give what I have received.

CHAPTER 4

Spiritual Warfare

DURING 2020, WHEN COVID HIT THE NATION, I TOOK A STEP BACK from pursuing real estate and started seeking God a lot more. I figured if I want to be successful in anything and want my family to have all their needs met, I need to focus on God and He will take care of us. He says in His word that we shouldn't worry about what we eat, drink, or wear.

"...For your heavenly Father knows that you need all these things. But seek first the kingdom of God and His righteousness, and all these things shall be added to you."
Matthew 6:32-33 NKJV

I started listening to the Bible through the Audible app and to sermons on YouTube. It got very annoying hearing all those ads, so I invested in my spiritual health by paying the YouTube premium plan; that way I could hear sermons and bible teachings while I was on the move. Ads were finally gone and I was able to learn from God without any distractions.

I came across this guy on YouTube talking about body, soul, and spirit. I was intrigued. I researched if soul and spirit were two different things. And this alone brought me to start my journey into learning what spiritual warfare was.

The word says in *1 Thessalonians 5:23 NKJV,* "*Now may the God of peace Himself sanctify you completely; and may your whole <u>spirit</u>, <u>soul</u>, <u>and body</u> be preserved blameless at the coming of our Lord Jesus Christ.*"

The fact that Paul mentioned these 3 things as uniquely different and not the same, made it more interesting. He is what I gathered so far, please give me grace on all this. I am still learning and I'm doing my best to be led by the Holy Spirit in learning. I don't know everything, I'm writing/typing this as I know it today. God will always continue to teach me, correct me, and help me understand as I seek Him.

Our Body

We obviously have a physical **body**, including what the body experiences, our senses and abilities.

- Taste
- Smell
- Vision
- Hearing
- Touch
- Speech/Communication (mainly speech and sign language)
- How we use our body (sex, physically hurt, sacrifice, suicide, lift someone up, etc.)

What we <u>see</u>, what we <u>hear</u>, and what you <u>touch</u>, affects who we become and our spiritual health. How we <u>communicate</u> can also affect ourselves, but can also affect others. From encouragement, to comfort, to loving others by your choice of words. But it can also tear down others and cause much pain through our words, or other ways of communication (like certain hand gestures using 1 finger). Then we have <u>how we use our bodies</u>. We can physically hurt or help someone. We can take our own lives as well as others. So what you do with your body can obviously affect who you are and will become as well as affect others in the process. We use all of our senses to learn and take part in this world.

Vision

We read books. We watch videos. We see how people interact. We see what people are affected by others' actions. We see pain. We see love. We experience the world through our eyes. We are traumatized if we see death or a loved one being hurt. We get scared when we watch a scary movie. Fear strikes you if you see a head peek out from your closet, then hides quickly. Be careful what you expose yourself to, and what is exposed to you and your children. Lust and perversion is always eager to step into your line of vision. We see how celebrities are treated and we want the same. So we seek to be noticed, appreciated, and praised. We show off what we have and what others don't. We envy others for what they have and what we don't. Do your best to control what you see and how you perceive things. If you have eyes to see, let them see. And what you are looking at may not always be what they seem. You know this. People can be fake. People act and people pretend. But most of all, we can use our vision to read the word of God for ourselves. We can see God's heart through His words. We can gain knowledge, wisdom and understanding, comfort, love, peace, joy from His word. From Jesus, who is His word made flesh. And with the right heart, a desire to understand, discernment, and God's gift of wisdom, you can see the truth in everything.

Hearing

We listen, we learn. We listen, apply to our lives the best we know how, and learn a few more things on the way to success. We also watch videos to learn, but it's still what is being said or taught that is important. We ask questions and the teacher or instructor will do their best to answer them. If we don't receive the information, we aren't able to start the process of learning.

If you hear hurtful words from your parents, a loved one, or even someone you don't know, it will undoubtedly affect you. You may try and brush it off if you have matured, but we are human and we interact with each other everyday. If you are listening to a person talk down and saying offending things to you long enough, you will either try to avoid them, hate them, resent them, get revenge, or even start to <u>believe</u> what they are saying. Same thing with music, if it's sad and depressing, you will start to sink deeper into feeling sad and depressed. If you listen to vulgar and sexualized music, your words will reflect them, as well as the way you think. Demons can enter doors you open by the things you listen to purposely and abide in. So just because someone drives by listening to music that is cursing or talking about how great it is to drink and take drugs, and you hear it for a few seconds doesn't mean demons will attach themselves onto you. Not saying they can't but is very unlikely. If you are abiding in Jesus and He is your Lord and Savior, and in your heart you reject and hate all evil, you are protected. If you listen to music praising or honoring God, you will most likely feel His peace, His joy, and His Holy Spirit. You will experience how He feels about you. You will begin to get a greater understanding of who He is and what He has done for others as well as allow you to realize what He has already done for you. So be cautious of what you are listening to.

If you ever hear a voice to hurt yourself or hurt others, understand, that is a demon. Your flesh is selfish, you want what is best for YOU. So hurting yourself isn't in the category of taking care of yourself, that's why it's a demon. They only want to steal, kill, and destroy your joy, peace, and life; along with your loved ones.

If you think you heard from God, ask His Holy Spirit for confirmation. Read His Word and ask Him to reveal something that matches with what you think you heard from Him. Ask Him for a dream. Go to the secret place and pray. Fast if you feel led to from the Holy Spirit. He will say things that demons will never say. You know you heard from God when even your flesh doesn't want to do; like give that homeless guy some food and you're not really feeling it. It takes time to get used to.

Want to grow your faith? Then **listen**, hear God's word, then do what it says.

"So then <u>faith comes by hearing</u>, and hearing by the word of God."
Romans 10:17 NKJV

"He replied, "<u>Blessed rather are those who hear the word of God and obey it</u>.""
Luke 11:28 NIV

"<u>Do not merely listen to the word</u>, and so deceive yourselves. <u>Do what it says</u>."
James 1:22 NIV

Touch & How we use our body

Some of us learn from hands on. We need to hold and use whatever we are being taught to do. Everything we do gets better with practice. If you go and practice witchcraft and use ouija boards, this will definitely affect your spiritual walk. And this ties into <u>how you use your body</u>. As I said before, using our body to hurt others or help saving someone's life is going to affect your spiritual walk. The Word explains how we are to act. Be kind, love one another, walk the extra mile, be merciful, have grace.

"But <u>love your enemies, do good, and lend, hoping for nothing in return</u>; and your reward will be great, and you will be sons of the Most High. For He is kind to the unthankful and evil."
Luke 6:35 NKJV

"And <u>be kind to one another, tenderhearted, forgiving one another</u>, even as God in Christ forgave you."
Ephesians 4:32 NKJV

"38 "You have heard that it was said, 'An eye for an eye and a tooth for a tooth.' 39 But I tell you not to resist an evil person. But <u>whoever slaps you on your right cheek, turn the other to him also</u>. 40 If anyone wants to sue you and take away your tunic, <u>let him have your cloak also</u>. 41 And whoever compels you to go one mile, <u>go with him two</u>. 42 <u>Give to him who asks you</u>, and from him who wants to borrow from you do not turn away. 43 "You have heard that it was said, 'You shall love your neighbor and hate your enemy.' 44 But I say to you, <u>love your enemies</u>, <u>bless those who curse you</u>, <u>do good to those who hate you</u>, and <u>pray for those who spitefully use you and persecute you</u>, 45 that you may be sons of your Father in heaven; for He makes His sun rise on the evil and on the good, and sends rain on the just and on the unjust."
Matthew 5:38-45 NKJV

Speech

The power of the tongue. What we say can hurt others or build them up. Agreeing with the enemy is building verbal agreements that will last your lifetime, and could affect your children and your children's children. What is seen is temporary and what is unseen is eternal. Think about a written contract, when a condition is met or someone passes away, most contracts go void. Now imagine the words of a parent spoken over their own child before they were even born. Saying things like, "I wish I had a boy." When the doctor told them it was a girl. A spirit of rejection now has access to enter that baby. Or when a person tells their child they will **never** make it, they **always** do this or that, these are spoken word curses. When we say these words, we are prophetically speaking over someone's life. It commonly happens when someone is in charge over another person. Teacher/Instructor over their students, Parents/Grandparents over their children, or any authoritative figure over another person. Age doesn't matter. It's just more common because they get frustrated or angry with the person they are caring for or overseeing. A child can walk up to their parents and say "You'll always be lazy!" or "You always yell at me!" Well demons don't care who spoke the words, they will honor what God has given us. He has given us power through our words. We need to help each other understand this and teach our children not to say such things, even if full grown adults still haven't learned to control their tongue. What comes out of our mouths is what defiles us.

"Not what goes into the mouth defiles a man; <u>but what comes out of the mouth, this defiles a man</u>."
Matthew 15:11 NKJV

"17 Do you not yet understand that whatever enters the mouth goes into the stomach and is eliminated? 18 But <u>those things which proceed out of the mouth come from the heart</u>, and they defile a man. <u>19 For out of the heart proceed evil thoughts, murders, adulteries, fornications, thefts, false witness, blasphemies</u>."
Matthew 15:17-19 NKJV

Here are other verses concerning our tongue and our words.

"2 Indeed, we all make many mistakes. <u>For if we could control our tongues, we would be perfect and could also control ourselves in every other way</u>. 4 And a small rudder makes a huge ship turn wherever the pilot chooses to go, even though the winds are strong. 5 In the same way,

the tongue is a small thing that makes grand speeches. But a tiny spark can set a great forest on fire. 6 And among all the parts of the body, but no one can tame the tongue. It is a whole world of wickedness, corrupting your entire body. It can set your whole life on fire, for it is set on fire by hell itself. 7 People can tame all kinds of animals, birds, reptiles, and fish, 8 but no one can tame the tongue. And so blessing and cursing come pouring out of the same mouth. 9 Sometimes it praises our Lord and Father, and sometimes it curses those who have been made in the image of God. 10 And so blessing and cursing come pouring out of the same mouth. Surely, my brothers and sisters, this is not right! 13 If you are wise and understand God's ways, prove it by living an honorable life, doing good works with the humility that comes from wisdom. 14 But if you are bitterly jealous and there is selfish ambition in your heart, don't cover up the truth with boasting and lying. 15 For jealousy and selfishness are not God's kind of wisdom. Such things are earthly, unspiritual, and demonic. 16 For wherever there is jealousy and selfish ambition, there you will find disorder and evil of every kind." 17 But the wisdom from above is first of all pure. It is also peace loving, gentle at all times, and willing to yield to others. It is full of mercy and the fruit of good deeds. It shows no favoritism and is always sincere. 18 And those who are peacemakers will plant seeds of peace and reap a harvest of righteousness."
James 3:2,4-10,13-18 NLT

"Let no corrupt communication proceed out of your mouth, but that which is good to the use of edifying, that it may minister grace unto the hearers."
Ephesians 4:29 KJV

"1 Therefore be imitators of God as dear children. 3 But fornication and all uncleanness or covetousness, let it not even be named among you, as is fitting for saints; 4 neither filthiness, nor foolish talking, nor coarse jesting, which are not fitting, but rather giving of thanks. 5 For this you know, that no fornicator, unclean person, nor covetous man, who

is an *idolater, has any inheritance in the kingdom of Christ and God.*
6 Let no one deceive you with empty words, for because of these things
the wrath of God comes upon the sons of disobedience. 7 Therefore do
not be partakers with them."
Ephesians 5:1,3-7 NKJV

"A person's words can be a source of wisdom, deep as the ocean, fresh as
a flowing stream."
Proverbs 18:4 GNT

"The soothing tongue is a tree of life, but a perverse tongue crushes the
spirit."
Proverbs 15:4 NIV

"Gracious words are a honeycomb, sweet to the soul and healing to the
bones."
Proverbs 16:24 NIV

"The thoughts of the wicked are an abomination to the Lord, But the
words of the pure are pleasant."
Proverbs 15:26 NKJV

"But now is the time to get rid of anger, rage, malicious behavior,
slander, and dirty language."
Colossians 3:8 NLT

So be careful what you say. Talk to God and say this…

"I said, 'I will guard my ways, that I may not sin with my tongue; I will
guard my mouth with a muzzle, so long as the wicked are in my presence.'"
Psalm 39:1 ESV

Speak blessings over others. We renounce our previous words
using our tongue. The demons hate it and it frees us from all

obligations we made with the devil and his minions. Jesus breaks every chain. When we speak over someone or something in Jesus NAME, it's as though we speak on His behalf. As though the King of Kings said it Himself.

People in the New Age movement think we can manifest things just by self affirming or proclaiming them out loud. "I will be rich! I will be rich! I will be rich!" But it stems off what the Bible says. Our words do have power, but the devil perverts it. We can speak blessing over something in Jesus name and believe it may come to pass, as long as it's according to His will. We can also speak evil, hurt, curses and that will also come to pass (if the other person isn't already protected by God and His angels) that's why we have to be careful. But know that any curse you put on someone else will come back onto you. Here is where people believe in Karma. And to a certain degree they are right but it isn't superstition or "karma", it's what God told us would happen.

"As I have observed, <u>those who plow evil</u> and those who sow trouble <u>reap it</u>."
Job 4:8 NIV

"Whoever digs a pit will fall into it; if someone rolls a stone, it will <u>roll back on them</u>."
Proverbs 26:27 NIV

"The trouble they cause recoils on them; <u>their violence comes down on their own heads</u>."
Psalm 7:16 NIV

"Do not be deceived: God cannot be mocked. <u>A man reaps what he sows</u>."
Galatians 6:7 NIV

"3 Do not drag me away with the wicked, with those who do evil, who speak cordially with their neighbors but harbor malice in their hearts.

4 <u>Repay them for their deeds and for their evil work; repay them for what their hands have done and bring back on them what they deserve.</u>"
Psalms 28:3-4 NIV

"Whoever seeks good finds favor, but evil comes to one who searches for it."
Proverbs 11:27 NIV

"Whoever closes his ear to the cry of the poor will himself call out and not be answered."
Proverbs 21:13 NIV

"Give, and it will be given to you. Good measure, pressed down, shaken together, running over, will be put into your lap. <u>For with the measure you use it will be measured back to you.</u>"
Luke 6:38 NIV

In summary, what you see, listen to, do, and say all have an impact on your spiritual life as well as other people. So we need to stay cautious, aware of the enemies' devices and pray for self-control.

Our Soul

We have a **soul**, which I believe is who we are as a person, a personality. This includes the way we think, our memories, experiences, knowledge, intelligence, wisdom, understanding, emotions, point of view, opinions, and our heart (which I believe is our will and deep desires). And based on who you are, what you know, why you feel a certain way about certain things, you will perceive a situation much different than others. God created us to have different personality traits. No person is exactly the same. Even twins who grow up in the same home, same environment, exposed to the same things, can have completely different perspectives and opinions.

Our hearts also have a sinful nature that comes with evil intentions and evil desires.

Which is why we say "our hearts' desire". This goes deeper as to what you want in life; money, fame, power, sex, drugs, acceptance, revenge, freedom, peace, joy, and much more. We all have an inner battle. Fighting against ourselves to do good, even though our fleshly desire & sinful nature wants to do wrong. Most of us don't want to put in the work. Most of us ultimately want to get to a place where we don't have to work as much and relax in retirement, however that may look like. And when we push ourselves to get up everyday and get to work, then we become disciplined and successful.

Unforgiveness in your heart can allow a demon to enter. Your deep thoughts about someone or something can open doors for demons to come in. Remember lust. It's just thoughts, but meditating on it can affect your soul. You become one with your thoughts, and if you allow yourself to have evil thoughts and NOT captivate them, you are pushing God away and pulling in evil.

"3 For though we walk in the flesh, we do not war according to the flesh. 4 For the weapons of our warfare are not carnal but mighty in God for pulling down strongholds, 5 casting down arguments and every high thing that exalts itself against the knowledge of God, bringing every thought into captivity to the obedience of Christ, 6 and being ready to punish all disobedience when your obedience is fulfilled."
2 Corinthians 10:3-6 NKJV

Our Spirit

Then there's our **spirit**. At birth we were born into a life of spiritual death because of sin. I believe we are all spiritually dead, destined to the lake of fire (hell), until we are spiritually born again through Christ, by believing in Jesus Christ and surrendering our lives to Him. As far as what our spirit completely consists of, I don't completely know. From scripture I see that we can pray in spirit because God is Spirit, but I have a lot to learn. I'll just share what I have experienced thus far.

Introduced to Spiritual Warfare

I know there are evil spirits, which are also called demons, because the bible mentions them. From what I have read and listened to, they are the spirits of the nephilim, being that they aren't fully human or fully angel. And because they were destroyed in the flood, their bodies are gone but their spirits roam the earth, searching for who to destroy according to the devil's plans.

As I began to read about the spiritual realm and where our fight begins and ends, I obviously found these verses.

10 Finally, my brethren, be strong in the Lord and in the power of His might. 11 Put on the whole armor of God, that you may be able to stand against the wiles of the devil. 12 For we do not wrestle against flesh and blood, but against principalities, against powers, against the rulers of the darkness of this age, against spiritual hosts of wickedness in the heavenly places. 13 Therefore take up the whole armor of God, that you may be able to withstand in the evil day, and having done all, to stand."
Ephesians 6:10-13 NKJV

We do not fight against flesh, the people physically in this world, we fight against spiritual hosts of evil in the heavenly "unseen" places. During this time, Delila sends me this other video concerning "Spiritual Warfare". The people talking were Isaiah Saldivar and John Ramirez. My eyes began opening up to the truth that's out there. I did not know what I was blind to all these years. Demons, spirits, angels, and more importantly, the Holy Spirit and His gifts for us. I learned about being baptized in the Holy Spirit and speaking in tongues was available to all believers.

I dove deep into everything Isaiah was teaching on his channel. In his videos I was introduced to Pastor Vladimir Savchuk and Apostle Alexander Pagani. Amazing men of God. On YouTube I also find Evangelist Daniel Adams and Marcus Rogers. These brothers in Christ, God would use them to help me shape my growth. Specifically Isaiah Saldivar and Vlad, I would learn about:

- Blessings vs Curses
- Generational Curses
- Soul Ties
- Spirit of Religion
- Jezebel/Lust spirits
- Python/Witchcraft spirits
- Witches & Warlocks
- Leviathan/Pride spirits
- Octopus/Mind control spirits
- Succubus & Incubus spirits
- Night/Dream spirits
- Astral Projection
- New Age Practices & Yoga
- Angels/Demons/Principalities/Fallen Angels/Nephilim
- Haunted Houses
- Accursed/Cursed items
- Contracts/Vows/Hexes/Pacts/Curses
- Animal spirits
- Anxiety & Depression spirits
- Anger & Wrath spirits
- Premature death, Suicide, & Death spirits
- Spirit of Infirmity/Physical pain or sickness
- Blind & Mute spirits
- Rebellious spirits
- Gay/Trans spirits
- How demons use unforgiveness to enter/stay
- How many evil spirits enter

- How to remove evil spirits/Cast out demons
- How to protect ourselves
- Healings
- Baptizing in the Holy Spirit
- Canceling contracts
- Speaking in tongues
- Abiding in Jesus
- Power in the name of Jesus Christ
- Who we are as Children of God
- The Secret Place
- Fasting & Praying
- God's Mercy & Grace
- Praising & Worshiping God
- Building our Faith & Fruit of the Holy Spirit
- Gifts of the Holy Spirit & how to use them
- Repenting and surrendering to God, Jesus, & the Holy Spirit

And there are so many sermons from both of these men of God that I learned from, cried from, grew from, and tried teaching my family about.

First House Deliverance

My brother, Vincent, and I began to pursue what God commanded us to do, and that's the Great Commission in *Mark 16:15-18.*

"15 And He said to them, 'Go into all the world and preach the gospel to every creature. 16 He who believes and is baptized will be saved; but he who does not believe will be condemned. 17 And these signs will follow those who believe: In My name they will cast out demons; they will speak with new tongues; 18 they will take up serpents; and if they drink

69

anything deadly, it will by no means hurt them; they will lay hands on the sick, and they will recover.'"
Mark 16:15-18 NKJV

My wife had a co-worker who mentioned she had some spiritual entities in her home. My wife told her about Vincent and I. She agreed for us to head over and pray over the home.

During the week, we call her and ask what was happening in the home. She explains the kids are scared to enter the upstairs living room. That a tall 8 ft skinny black figure with long fingers would scare the kids.

Saturday morning comes, Vincent and I head out to the home. When we get there, we pray in the car. We knock on the door and the discernment begins. Vincent can discern more than I can. So I know he will feel it before I can. We walk around the first floor not really sensing anything scary or eerie. When we get to the top step of the stairs, everything changes. Vincent immediately feels darkness. I didn't discern anything until we walked about 10 ft, to the entrance of the hallway. It seemed like the hallway got longer and darker as you just stood there.

We mention what we feel and they confirm, saying that the tall figure would walk around the hallway and enter the living room. We walk into the living room and it feels like we just entered a haunted eerie room filled with darkness and evil. They also tell us there is this dark, purple cloud-like spirit at the corner of that room. We tell them we are going to pray and we'll tell them when we are done.

My brother and I look at each other with a bit of astonishment that we are actually here and there are evil spirits tormenting this family. We jump right into praying. He's praying in tongues. I ask God to cleanse the home of all evil spirits. We both demand all demons to leave that home and to never return. We ask the Holy Spirit to fill the home with His presence. We continue this until we don't feel any demonic presence in the room. Then we went into the hallway.

We continue this process throughout the entire home, entering every room, with permission of course. When we get downstairs we speak to some of the people living there. The owner's daughter tells us she can see evil spirits. When she is at home in another state, she can see into this house and see demons floating over her Mom. She described it as black hair entangled within itself, moving in a ball spinning manner. We ask them if they'd like us to pray over them after the house is cleansed, and they agree.

Once we are done with the downstairs, we head back up. The kids ran past us into the living room. The owner is surprised and tells us this isn't normal. The kids hated being in that room and now they are just running around without any problems.

Before we start praying with them, we ask questions of past sins they have committed dealing with ouija boards, psychics, palm readings, witchcraft and anything that would come to mind. The pregnant daughter tells us she has had dreams about a demon telling her that the baby was his. And even had a picture of an ultrasound with the demon's face on it. It was very creepy. We tell her we'll pray with her as well.

As we start praying over the owner, she is crying and feeling peace. We pray over her daughter, who isn't pregnant. And she begins to shake and manifest. Vincent gets bolder as the Holy Spirit uses him to speak against the demonic presence. But the demon didn't speak or get casted out. I get a work of knowledge and ask if she has unforgiveness. She agrees and says she doesn't know how to forgive that person. We begin to guide her that God will help her forgive if she is willing. That she isn't alone in this but she has to want to and let God change her heart. We finish the prayer.

We find out the pregnant daughter leaves with her family quickly. Almost as if she was led away from us, so we wouldn't pray over her. We still prayed from afar but we believe God will help her through it.

Vincent and I leave and discuss what happened that day. We talk about what we could have done differently. How amazing God is with all His peace, grace, mercy, and power. We felt so alive and bold, and had a fire to help those in need again. That night and the following day, we were so exhausted. It really took a lot out of us. Now we know why Jesus told His disciples to eat when they were explaining all that they did in His name. We may get excited and caught up in delivering people but we are still human and need to rest for the next round of demon fighting.

The Second House Visit

My wife posted a bible verse about God's mercy and power. Her co-worker sees it and reaches out to her. She remembers what she previously said about Vincent and I learning Spiritual Warfare. She invites us to visit and check out her home.

We head over and examine her home. Only thing I felt was in their closet. When I stepped into the master bedroom's closet, this dark presence was there. I prayed over it and it was gone. We get downstairs and I ask about the closet and she is surprised that I noticed something there. She said she wasn't sure if something was there or not. Just felt creeped out by it. But I reassured her that there isn't anything there now.

When we speak to the entire family, Mom, Dad, their son and daughter about Jesus Christ and His wonders, their daughter mentioned pain in her neck. That she always has this pain on her right side of her neck. We asked if it was ok to pray over her. We had the Mom touch her daughter's neck and we prayed. The daughter felt the pain go down a bit. So we pray again. Again she felt less pain, but still there. So we pray one more time. Her face changes to full excitement and looks straight at her Mom and says, "The pain is gone!" Praise God!

Times like this are so amazing. That God uses us to heal each other and to love one another.

Electricity

I got a call from a person who found me on Isaiah's Deliverance Map. I'm on the freeway heading home after work. As this guy tells me about pain he feels in his abdomen, I began thinking of ways to meet this person so I can pray over him. I told him I don't know what my schedule looks like but I can pray right now over the phone.

He agrees and I begin to pray over his body, and his stomach pain. I ask, "How does it feel now?" He said it's a lot less painful. We pray again and the same thing, less pain but not completely gone. He shifted to saying his right ankle was hurting too. I pray that the spirit of infirmity leaves and God will heal him. He begins laughing.

I am so confused at this point. Was this guy just joking around or was he being serious? He tells me that he felt electricity run down his leg and to his ankle, then proceeds to say he feels no more pain! I told him this is wild. I know God can do these things, but it's still so surprising that it happened. AND over the phone! Wow. God is so good. He meets you where you're at. He has no limits. He is the Almighty God. All praise and worship belongs to Him.

There are other stories and much more to come. But if you want more of these, go check out Daniel Adams and his team at The Supernatural Life aka TSNL. As well as Apostle Alexander Pagani.

Thank God I Got Covid

In 2020, on Thanksgiving Day, I tested positive for Covid-19. The next few days, I really felt hopeless. Viewing myself as a useless person. I began to think no matter how hard I try to support my family or enjoy time with friends and family, what was the point? Everything is pointless. Everyone is going to die eventually. No matter how hard working I can be, it isn't going to benefit anyone.

Of course I got most of the symptoms that comes with having Covid. The body aches, fever, loss of taste and smell, weakness, headaches, tiredness, loss of appetite, hard time breathing, chest pain, and the vulnerable parts you already suffer from get worse. In my case, I pulled my upper back while in the military. And when covid hit me, my upper back was in so much pain.

The more I read about how others felt during their time with Covid-19, the more I believe it's a spiritual attack more than it is a physical attack on the body. The entire world is afraid. People are going out of control because of the fear of getting covid. And those who got covid, they claim to have suicidal thoughts, thoughts of uselessness just like I experienced.

A week passes and I get this intense headache. I get so mad I blame God. I say, "God, I thought You loved me. I thought You were going to protect me from this. I am Your son. Why am I going through this!?"

God tells me, "You said you'd trust me through anything. You thought you had great faith. You said you would praise me through any circumstance and that you'd trust me. But notice how you are reacting to this trial."

"God, I'm sorry. You're right. I thought I had great faith. Thank You for showing me this. Next time I run into a sickness, great pain, or trial, I will think twice about how I react. Thank You for giving me Covid so that my faith may grow, as well as my trust in You."

God Responses to My Wife

Less than a month later, my wife's parents get covid. They face breathing complications and are taken to the hospital. My wife is trying her best to hold herself together. She prays and enters a fast. She then asks God if He can tell her how her parents are going to do. A hope of a future of their health.

The following day, I woke up and told her I had a dream. I told her that my dream took place in her parent's living room and both her parents were sitting and relaxing as we went to visit them. They were healthy and having a great time with us and their grandchildren.

My wife tells me she prayed for God to give her a dream or a sign that her parents were going to be ok. And that God gave me the dream. Maybe to ensure to her that it wasn't her making it up.

A few days pass, the doctors are amazed by how quickly her parents were recovering. They were out of the hospital within a week in which they entered. The doctors say, "For their age group, the average stay in the hospital is about 2-3 weeks." It was truly a blessing from God.

On Christmas day, we all sat around in my in-laws' home. Suddenly I remembered my dream. We all sat there similarly to how it was in the dream. I begin to tear up as I see what God has shown me and how His grace is so great. We don't deserve to be here, enjoying ourselves. But we are, because He is good. All glory to God and His healing power. He is our hope and peace.

I Finally Pray in Tongues

I want to share my story of how I finally was able to pray in tongues, something I thought I could never do. And this doubt I held, was one of the reasons why I couldn't pray in tongues sooner. I knew that speaking in tongues was a gift of the Holy Spirit in *1 Corinthians 12.*

"to another the working of miracles, to another prophecy, to another discerning of spirits, to another <u>different kinds of tongues</u>, to another the interpretation of tongues."
1 Corinthians 12:10 NKJV

From what I have learned, there are two ways of speaking in tongues. One is in public, where speaking in tongues is in these different languages which happened in *Acts 2.*

"And they were all filled with the Holy Spirit and began to <u>speak with other tongues</u>, as the Spirit gave them utterance."
Acts 2:4 NKJV

"And when this sound occurred, the multitude came together, and were confused, because <u>everyone heard them speak in his own language</u>."
Acts 2:6 NKJV

When this happens and we speak in different languages, it's so that the gospel can be preached to all the nations. God gives us a way to communicate to places where we don't know the native language. Now let's look at another way speaking in tongues was explained by Paul.

"If anyone speaks in a tongue, let there be two or at the most three, each in turn, and let one interpret. But if there is no interpreter, let him keep silent in church, and let him speak to himself and to God."
1 Corinthians 14:27-28 NKJV

This doesn't mention different languages, but a tongue where interpretation is needed when speaking to a congregation. If there is no interpreter, Paul is saying to keep silent in church, as in out loud for all to hear, for it doesn't edify others, but go ahead and pray in tongues to yourself and to God. So this second way is speaking in tongues in an unknown heavenly language, whether to a congregation with interpretation, or between you and God.

We can still pray in tongues whenever we want but to be careful of the whole church doing it all at once and confusing the unbelievers. In conclusion, we have:

1. Different languages with no need of interpretation, as everyone will hear their own language.
    2a. Unknown heavenly language in need of interpretation if speaking out to a congregation.

   2b. Unknown heavenly language praying to God, edifying
      yourself.

"He who speaks in a tongue doesn't talk to men but to God."
1 Corinthians 14:2 NKJV

"He who speaks in a tongue edifies himself."
1 Corinthians 14:4 NKJV

If you want to speak in tongues with no intention of speaking to the people, but only to our Father, this is simply praying in tongues, praying in the Spirit. In Jude it says to build ourselves up on our most holy faith, praying in the Holy Spirit.

"But you, beloved, building yourselves up on your most holy faith, praying in the Holy Spirit,"
Jude 1:20 NKJV

This shows us that praying in the Holy Spirit is for all. There are no restrictions. He didn't say, IF you can pray in the Holy Spirit but to build yourselves up on your faith by praying in the Holy Spirit. And reading *Mark 16*, I believe that all who believe in Jesus Christ will speak with new tongues.

"15 And He said to them, 'Go into all the world and preach the gospel to every creature. 16 He who believes and is baptized will be saved; but he who does not believe will be condemned. 17 And these signs will follow those who believe: In My name they will cast out demons; they will speak with new tongues; 18 they will take up serpents; and if they drink anything deadly, it will by no means hurt them; they will lay hands on the sick, and they will recover.'"
Mark 16:15-18 NKJV

So why don't I speak in new tongues? I believe and I'm baptized. Aren't I?...

"2 he said to them, "Did you receive the Holy Spirit when you believed? "So they said to him, "We have not so much as heard whether there is a Holy Spirit." 3 And he said to them, "Into what then were you baptized?" So they said, "Into John's baptism." 4 Then Paul said, "John indeed baptized with a baptism of repentance, saying to the people that they should believe on Him who would come after him, that is, on Christ Jesus." 5 When they heard this, they were baptized in the name of the Lord Jesus. 6 And when Paul had laid hands on them, the Holy Spirit came upon them, and they spoke with tongues and prophesied."
Acts 19:2-6 NKJV

Paul asks these men if they had received the Holy Spirit when they believed. If Paul asked me this question, I wouldn't know how to answer. How would I know if I received the Holy Spirit? Then he goes on to explain we need to be baptized by the Lord Jesus, and when he laid hands on them, they got baptized with the Holy Spirit, and spoke in new tongues. Now I'm doubting I was ever even baptized in the Holy Spirit. But I was determined to make sure I was.

I hop on a live zoom call with Daniel Adams. I'm desperate for the Lord and I asked to be filled with the Holy Ghost. He prays over me and I feel this very small warm spot in my chest. He proceeds to tell me to speak in tongues as evidence of my baptism and faith. I try my best, but it just feels like I'm just saying gibberish. This can't be it. I feel like it's me doing it. He affirms to me that it is tongues. I rebuke any doubt in me and go for it. I say to myself, "I am filled with the Holy Spirit and I do speak in tongues." And with that step of faith, I fully embrace my prayer language. Finally I speak in tongues!

My doubt was holding me back. And it all makes sense why most people don't try it or believe it can happen to them. It's just faith that activates what you already have. I now believe, every believer who is filled with the Holy Spirit (aka baptized in the Holy Spirit) can speak in tongues. Pride, doubt, or feeling unworthy stops your tongues. This is a gift I have been praying for but never understood I already had it when I was baptized awhile back. My family said I showed the fruit of the Holy Spirit in my life, so I already had the Holy Spirit. But it was my doubt and insecurity that blocked my prayer language. If you want to speak in tongues, accept Jesus as Lord and Savior, be baptized in our Lord Jesus Christ and be filled with the Holy Spirit. Then by faith, speak in your prayer language. This is a free gift from God. We don't earn it, we don't deserve it. Just accept it and allow Him to change you from the inside out, in His timing.

Next I'm working on prophesying. Lord teach me how to prophecy as this edifies the church.

"3 But he who prophesies speaks edification and exhortation and comfort to men. 4 He who speaks in a tongue edifies himself, but he who prophesies edifies the church. 5 I wish you all spoke with tongues, but even more that you prophesied; for he who prophesies is greater than he who speaks with tongues, unless indeed he interprets, that the church may receive edification."
1 Corinthians 14:3-5 NKJV

Now 2023 is here and my faith is over the top! If I pray over anyone and I believe they will get healed. Though I fight myself on walking over to a complete stranger, I believe if I actually pray for them (and possibly lay hands) they WILL get healed. But of course doubt likes to creep in and say, "Well what if it doesn't happen? And God will be misrepresented?" I pray God continues to increase my boldness, as well as my discernment to know when someone needs prayer, and a sensitive ear to hear His voice.

CHAPTER 5

God Speaks (Dream House Testimony)

Now that I was all settled into my first home, I began to research how I can benefit from it. I found the BRRRR method (Buy, Renovate, Rent, Refinance, & Repeat). I would listen to the Bigger Pockets Podcast and try to find ways to use my property as leverage to create income streams. Maybe I can rent it out and make some rental income, or refinance it to buy something investable. But I didn't know what to do. I got to the point where I didn't care what happened. Whether we stay at this house, make it a rental property, or sell it on the market. I knew God would guide us on which way to go.

One day, I began to talk to God and ask random questions in the shower. We all ask God questions and usually we don't get an answer right at that moment; so we get used to God not responding right? Of course some people do and I hope to get there one day.

I ask, "God should we rent this house? Should we sell it? Or should we continue to live here? God I don't care if we have to live here forever as long as You are with us and protecting us. So if we should rent this house, when should we start the process; if we should sell, when should we sell and buy the new home; and if You want us to stay here, for how long?"

Immediately I hear, "Sell." I was not expecting God to speak so clearly. And for a moment my skeptical mind thinks maybe I thought this. Then I hear something, "Look at the numbers." This clearly wasn't me. I'm surprised I just heard God. He knows I'm analytical. He knew this would reassure me on why He said to sell our home.

I jumped out of the shower and told my wife, "I think God just told me we should sell our house. I asked Him if we should rent, sell, or stay here, and He told me 'sell', and 'look at the numbers'." So we began to write the numbers on our fridge whiteboard. How much our home could potentially sell for, how much houses were on the market for, interest rates, and so on.

Market Crashes Scenario

We created a scenario as if the market crashed 1 year from then, and what that would mean for our sale. Interest rates would be much higher because houses have dropped in value. We would sell low causing us to have less money in our pocket, but it would also mean we would buy low. But with the market in this day and age, you would still need to put more money upfront to beat out the competition. There would be more competition than there was in 2008-2009. So we would have to beat out cash buyers, investors, and people who have been waiting for this exact moment for so long. And people who sold their home expecting this crash, would have to buy whatever deal came their way, even if it was a bad deal. Not understanding it would cost them more than they thought.

After some calculations, it would cost more per month with a crash than if there was no crash. Why? Because even if housing increased by 25% over the next year, and a crash did occur, housing would drop around 25%, making it the same price it is today BUT with a higher interest rate. Resulting in a higher monthly payment. In conclusion, it's not worth selling our home after a crash, or even trying to predict a crash and sell too early.

Now on the other side, if we sell soon, we would have to buy high but we would also sell high, get a decent interest rate and have a hefty savings account. We said, "It's better to sell now while value is high, and purchase a home while interest rates are still low." Overall, this was much better. No wonder God told us to look at the numbers, it all made sense. From this moment forward, we focused on getting the house ready for sale.

A month later, in Jan 2021, I told Delila maybe the hefty savings that we'll obtain from the sale, is meant for me to pursue real estate full time. And she said, "Oh yea, maybe." The following day, God corrected me. He told me this money wasn't for me to pursue real estate, but for my wife to quit her job and focus on our kids. When I told Delila what happened, she told me this was confirmation of what was stirring in her heart. God put it in her heart to want to stay home but she was waiting on confirmation to make sure it wasn't her flesh wanting this. This also told me that I was to stay at my job, which is what I didn't want to hear.

Months pass as we prepare the house; changing doors, painting walls, fixing minor discrepancies, and organizing the garage. One weekend, my brother comes over and asks what else are we going to do to the home before he takes pictures for the MLS listing. I tell him I'm thinking about putting grass in the backyard for greater appeal. Or at least leveling out the dirt, because the dogs dug some holes. Then he asks if the backyard was nice when we first bought the home. I told him it actually looks the same. And then mentions if we bought it the way it was, why would it deter other people. I replied, "That is a great point. Forget the backyard. Let's take pictures next weekend." Pictures were taken, listing agreement was signed, and the house was placed on the market. I teamed up with another agent from my office in order to learn the process, as this was my first listing. For the sake of their identity, I'll say his name is Ryan. He was going to deal with the buyers and the Buyer's agent.

Buyers came to our open house, offers were placed, and after some negotiating, we entered escrow with a buyer. After 1 day, we lose the buyer. We couldn't believe it because we just put an offer on a beautiful home. We quickly respond to the other buyers, and enter escrow once again. During this week, my wife saw a TikTok video of a woman who goes to a house she was trying to purchase, and prays to get the house while she stands in the driveway. This lady was trespassing but she was bold about it. So we decided to do the same. We drove to the house, we placed our foot on the lawn, and prayed that if this house is meant to be ours, let His will be done. But we also prayed, if this house is not part of His plan for our family's life, don't let us have it Lord. People were probably watching us and thinking we were weird for doing this, but faith moves mountains. And we gotta be bold if we are to ask our heavenly Father for anything.

We get the call, we don't get the house. They say it's because we were contingent on selling our home, plus our competition offered more money. Mind you, during this time, people were putting offers well over listing prices; up to $50-60K over. It's a unpredictable market we are in, and if we are going to get an acceptance, it's going to be with God's help.

Almost 2 months pass as we continue to put offers left and right, but all rejected due to the same reasons. We weren't being conservative. I was doing my part on researching the values of these homes and putting offers accordingly, but we still got rejected every time. It got very discouraging, but we trusted God in what He was doing and for His reasons alone.

On a Thursday afternoon, Ryan tells me about this property our Broker just listed. I look at the pictures of the home and think, "Wow, this house looks amazing! And it has 5 Bedrooms and a pool!" Once I saw the city name, I figured, "Well no wonder it's up for sale. It's probably on that side of the town where the houses look decent but they still don't have the greatest schools and neighborhoods."

The next day, I tell my wife, Delila, "Let's go check out this house." She agrees and we all head out. When I put the address into Google Maps, it's pointing to the unknown part of town we weren't familiar with. We get there, and it blows our minds. The neighborhood is awesome. The house looked amazing. It seemed as if it came out of a magazine. The schools associated with the area were great. It was truly a dream home for us and our kids.

I look up the open house dates, and they are scheduled the following weekend. I tell Delila, "Let's put an offer." She agrees but says, "I thought you said sellers aren't accepting blind offers. Plus the house is going to show next weekend, won't they just say wait until after the open house?" I reply, "That's true most sellers don't want offers without the buyers seeing the house first, but who knows, maybe these sellers won't mind. I'll just ask if we can put in an offer. Worst case scenario, my boss will just tell me to wait until after the open house." She said ok.

I called my Broker, who is also the listing agent for the property. I asked him if we could place a blind offer, and to my surprise, he said, "Go for it." So we put an offer together and sent it over that Friday night. The next day, he calls me and says that they are actually considering our offer, and they will discuss it more in their meeting on Monday. This isn't happening. All the offers we placed on other homes were rejected and these sellers are actually considering our offer. They can just wait 1 more week and get 30 other offers, probably much better than ours. AND it's blind! Some sellers get upset when they receive these kinds of offers.

Monday rolls up, Delila is sitting down and I'm pacing. I got the call. "Hey man, they decided to go with someone else." I'm immediately confused. How come he didn't mention another person putting in an offer? After a brief silence, he says, "No, I'm kidding. They accepted your offer." And he laughs a bit. I replied laughing, "Aww man why did you say that? I was so confused, like who else could it be. Wow! This is wild." He congratulates us and explains we will be opening escrow tomorrow.

The Disbelief

I just can't believe it. I tell Delila in unbelief, "We got it. Our offer got accepted!" We both are in awe of what is happening. Are we dreaming? I better not wake up and it's Monday morning. I go to our bedroom and thank God. I continue to tell Delila that it doesn't feel real yet. The way we had our offer accepted was unfathomable. I mean this house is about to have an open house, in ONLY 1 week. We put in a BLIND offer. We put an offer less desirable than other offers we previously gave out due to the budget we're on. AND IT STILL GETS ACCEPTED? Everyone else just outright rejected us, or countered, and when we accepted their counter, they still chose someone else. In the market we are in today, this is a miracle. Thank you Lord! Now we know why it took this long, His perfect timing is incredible.

I headed over to the house to see it in person, as the sellers wanted to make sure we knew what we were getting into. When I walked inside, it was bigger than what was perceived in the photos online. I still don't believe it.

With research on the home value, we placed an offer accordingly. We understood you don't go off the listed price when putting an offer, you need to find out what the house is worth, the home value. Then you place an offer above the value to beat out the competition. If other buyers had good agents, they are going to tell their clients to place what the house is actually worth because the bank will pay up to that amount. But more experienced agents will tell their clients to place an offer even higher, along with good terms, to get a fighting chance. Even though we were ok with losing a good chunk of money to get the home, God made it where we didn't lose a penny. The Appraisal came back exactly what we offered. This blew my mind. God is so good. He is our Father and will always watch your back. Could this get any better.

After about 3 weeks of inspections, negotiating repairs, and a possible scam from a termite company, we got through it. Now we are at the finish line, with 1 week to go and everything is going smoothly, we were about to close.

Why God? Why?

On a Wednesday, with 1 day left before we close escrow on both homes, we lose our buyers. We get a call from Ryan. He says that the buyers' loan officer was verifying their job history and a discrepancy popped up. When they investigated, there was a gap in job history and reasoning was not justified. They claimed it was a temporary lay off due to covid, but come to find out, they "quit" for a few months. This disqualified them for their loan, and they were gone. Just like that.

I knew what this could mean, we lose our buyers, we lose the sellers. Why would they wait around for us to find another buyer, then wait another 30-45 days for their escrow to close? And that's saying nothing goes wrong,… again.

That evening, I fell to my knees crying out to God, "Please don't take this home from my family. They deserve it. I don't. Please God if it's anything I did wrong, please don't let my family be punished for it. Why God? What is happening? I thought this was the house You blessed us with. The way we got it was a miracle. But now that the buyers are gone, what could we possibly do to hang on to it? Please God guide me. Help us. Please allow us to get this home." God didn't respond.

When it got dark, we headed to the property and prayed over it. We prayed, "God if You want us to have this home, it will be ours, but if it isn't meant to be ours, God don't let us have it. Let Your will be done Lord. In Jesus name. Amen."

The next day, which was Thursday, I had to break this news to my broker/listing agent of our dream home. I called him and told him what had happened. He let us know that he was concerned that the sellers wouldn't stay with us. My heart dropped even though I expected he would say that. He said he'd try to figure something out. I talked to my loan officer and told him what happened and he gave encouraging words to hang in there and trust God.

What Are You Going To Do?

I was feeling pretty down. I sat at work thinking about what I could have done differently. Thinking if there is something I did wrong.

God asks me, "Why are you sad? Is that house even yours? What if I don't give it to you and your family? What are you going to do? Do you want to take control? If you try, understand that you will quickly ask Me to take over again."

And I reply, "Your right God. It isn't my house. You decide what will happen and what doesn't happen. If you don't give it to us, then I guess I will keep looking and trust You, that You know what's best for us. God... take it. I don't want it. I don't need that house. I only want what You want. You will give us what You believe is good and in Your timing."

Father and Son

Then He gives me this illustration. There is a Father and a son playing a card game vs another person. The son is behind the Father watching how the game is played. The son sees the play in front and doesn't fully understand. The Father tells the son, "Play this card." The son believes if he plays this card, they may lose but he trusts his Father. So he plays the card, they win overwhelmingly.

And God says, "What if you were in this game and you didn't play the card but held onto it? You would have lost. You would have remained where you were, in life, in struggle, in pain, in small blessings. Now let's take it a step further, and say that it costs you something valuable to play that card. And I tell you to give that thing up, to 'play that card'. Most people won't give it up, but hang on to it, they idolize it, or it's their security. They trust in it more than they do Me. They won't give up the control over their lives but cling on to it. But others, let go and trust Me as their Father and greater things come as a result. When I say to let go of something, I am trying to bless them with something better. But the wicked only see it as something being taken away."

The Legos

Another way I interpreted this lesson was a Father and son playing with Legos. The son is building a house and is so proud of his effort. The Father steps in and says, "Destroy it." The son is confused and the Father says, "Do you trust me?" The boy says, "Yes, Dad. I trust you." And the boy destroys what he has built. Then the Father steps in and gives his son more legos to build a bigger and cooler house. Then the boy is excited and glad he did what his Father had told him. If the boy didn't obey the Father, he would be in a place where he'd thought was his limit, possibly even blaming God for not allowing him to get further or overcoming something painful in his life. But when God tells us to let go of something, understand, it's for our own good.

The Comeback

Friday morning comes around. I talk to my broker and we devise a plan on getting my house back on the market and conduct an open house ASAP. We will get with the sellers and see if they're willing to wait based on this information, and how quickly we will try and close this new buyer escrow.

On Monday morning, my broker called and was surprised to tell me that the sellers were willing to wait. I thanked God for what was happening. Delila told me she believes this is God's way of telling us, what He has meant to be ours, will be ours. And wanted us to really believe this was from Him. There is no more denying that this house is from God Himself.

We find a new buyer, we go through the entire process and close escrow on our house. A day later, we closed escrow on the new house! This was a rollercoaster but we finally got the house. We scheduled a U-haul truck for the Saturday move-in. Friday afternoon, I get a call from the Sellers. They tell me they still haven't received their money and are concerned why. We talk to escrow and my Boss at the office and come to find out, the wiring instructions were inputted incorrectly. Whether the sellers wrote a wrong number or it was typed in wrong by the clerk. Either way, they weren't getting their money, they weren't happy and they wouldn't leave the house for us to move in, until they got their money.

The office did what they could and gave them a check of the full amount. Sellers took the check to the bank but the bank couldn't take it, being that it was too much. Sellers call me and say they are thinking of waiting until Tuesday to give us the keys, so that they have enough time for the funds to show up in their account on Monday. I'm just pacing back and forth, praying that the bank tells them exactly what they want to hear. While on the phone with them, bank guy comes over and tells them, the check clears out and hands them a confirmation. All glory to God.

Sellers tell me they still need a couple things to move and will give me the keys Saturday evening. I immediately let them know I have a U-haul first thing in the morning to move our things in and I offered to help them move out that night. They agreed. I head over to the new house and help them move. Meanwhile, the buyers agent of my old house was blowing me up about his buyers and when they could move in. I told him, we need time to move our stuff out and into our new home, as well as clean up for the new owners. We would hand over keys Sunday evening or Monday afternoon. He understood and relayed the message to his buyers.

Got the Keys!

As the sellers drove away and keys in hand, I couldn't believe it. We got the house! I feel like I'm in a dream. I turn around and stare at the house. "God You did this. There is no way that this was us, or even the people that were involved. We thank You for this blessing." I call my wife and tell her we got the keys. She is so excited and gets kids ready to come over. Remember, they never saw the house in person. She lets her parents know and they are also heading on over. During this entire journey of getting this house, we never showed them pictures, the address, or even what it completely had. We kept it a secret. As they're coming, I walk around the house, praying over every window, doorway, and outside perimeter. I dedicate this house to the Lord. I open this house to the Holy Spirit and to do whatever He wants, when He wants. As I walked around the empty house, I just felt complete peace.

About 10 minutes later, my wife shows up with the kids. I open the door and give them a tour. My wife is amazed and the kids are running around excited. Her parents showed up and couldn't believe what they saw. As it got later into the night, we went back to the old house, grabbed a couple of things, including our dogs and brought it all to the new house and slept there that night.

The next morning, we all worked together to pack the boxes into the U-haul and began the big move. 2 truck loads, a standoff with some pitbulls and a lunch later we were almost done. I get a call from the buyers' agent telling me they are eager to move in. I tell him again, we are almost done moving out and we will be cleaning the house all of Sunday. He tells me the buyers are on edge and may go to the old house. I tell him that the only way they can get the keys any sooner, is if we get all our stuff out that night and in the morning we clean up quickly. He says the buyers don't care about the cleaning, they want to move in already. I tell this to my in-laws and wife. I say, "We could bust a mission and head back for the rest of our stuff tonight, but we would have to use the cars (since we didn't have the U-haul anymore). The buyers are ok with us not cleaning it." My Father-in-law insists we do it and take the offer of not having to clean. So we agree.

Front Yard Camping

We get 3 cars ready and head back to the old house. When we get there, we thought there was a party going on nearby because of all the cars parked in the street. We reverse into the driveway. We get out of the cars and see all of the buyers camping out on the lawn. Their sofas, boxes, other furniture, stuff just piled up on the lawn. This was chaotic. I look at the buyers' agent with unbelief. He approaches me and apologizes for what was happening. I told them we will get our stuff and go. They try and ask if they could move their stuff in while we get our stuff out and I refuse. I tell them to wait and that it may take a couple of hours. They grunt and complain under their breath.

We begin to load the cars and my suv. As we walked around the house, I looked out my master bedroom and saw that they broke through our side gate and kicked down my kids' playhouse. I got mad but also knew I was going to leave it behind for them to keep. So in essence, they kicked down their own property. But if I was planning on taking it? They just kicked it down with no mercy on my kids' things. Anyways, I cooled off and just wanted to get out of there. As we loaded the last things, I took a video of the house completely messy. I wanted to have proof that they were accepting it in the condition that it was in. My wife made them a welcome home care package with a card. I close and lock the door behind me and walk towards them with this basket. I give them the basket and let them know my wife made it for them and we hope the house blesses them as it did us. I ask them again, are they sure they want to accept the house in the condition that it is in, it's very dirty and we were planning on cleaning it thoroughly on Sunday. They said they accept and that they would like to clean it. I say okayyyyyy. Then I hand them the keys, get into the car, drive away and never looked back. It felt like I was leaving an old life behind and was moving onto another chapter. It was a night to remember.

The next day, we begin to unpack and start our new chapter in our new dream home. I told my loan officer what happened the night prior and he was shocked. He said he believes it was the enemy kicking and screaming for what was happening. They wanted to make what was supposed to be a beautiful moment into a horrible experience. But it didn't work. We just brushed it off and enjoyed what God had given us. He also told me that we got the lowest interest rate there has been in the last 50 years (And we didn't even buy any points). And that's it, that's our dream house testimony.

This really amazed us with what God has done for us. I tell this story to all my friends, family, co-workers, and pretty much anyone who has doubts in what God can do. I first tell them about my marriage testimony, but most people just say, "Good for you." But for some reason, when I also share this, they are completely in awe of what God can do and how He sustained us through it all. I can prove it by showing them pictures and the data. My relationship with my wife is proof. My home is proof. And there is more to come.

Trust God in everything. Ask Him questions, and one day He will answer. But obey what He says and repent of your old ways. Read the Word of God as it will bring you truth. Let Him change your heart and your mind. He will help you work through your problems, which most are actually doorways into your breakthrough and soon, your testimony. He is a good God, so let Him show you.

CHAPTER 6

Prayer

PRAYER, THE MOST POWERFUL ACT IN HUMANITY. WE, THE creations, are given the ability to talk to God directly. When we pray, He hears us instantaneously. Isn't this hard to believe?

Jesus says your Father knows what you need before you ask Him, *Matthew 6:8*. So even before you speak, God knows. This isn't for us not to pray because He already knows, but to understand He is there, He knows what's in your heart. He understands you and knows what you need, even when we don't. Prayer is powerful. We are given this gift of direct communication, but we take it for granted. If we somehow earned this right, by some spiritual awakening, and it was the hardest thing we ever had to do, to be able to talk to GOD Himself, I believe we would never stop. And we would be teaching others how to do the same. And those who don't take it for granted and pour all of their time and energy into praying, God sees their unselfish, pure hearts and strongholds begin to crumble. So open your heart, say these scriptures out loud as children to our Father in heaven. Pour out your praise, your thanksgiving, your concerns, your worries, your tears, your hurt, your heart, your joy, your plead for others, your victory over the enemy because of His Son, and know that He will answer you one way or another. Ask for His mercy, grace, patience, tolerance, freedom, love, peace, joy, strength, protection, and guidance.

"Hear me when I call, O God of my righteousness! You have relieved me in my distress; Have mercy on me, and hear my prayer."
Psalms 4:1 NKJV

"Give ear to my words, O Lord, Consider my meditation. Give heed to the voice of my cry, My King and my God, For to You I will pray. My voice You shall hear in the morning, O Lord; In the morning I will direct it to You, And I will look up."
Psalms 5:1-3 NKJV

"But know that the Lord has set apart for Himself him who is godly; The Lord will hear when I call to Him."
Psalms 4:3 NKJV

"I will praise You, O Lord, with my whole heart; I will tell of all Your marvelous works. I will be glad and rejoice in You; I will sing praise to Your name, O Most High."
Psalms 9:1-2 NKJV

"Depart from me, all you workers of iniquity; For the Lord has heard the voice of my weeping. The Lord has heard my supplication; The Lord will receive my prayer."
Psalms 6:8-9 NKJV

"O Lord my God, if I have done this: If there is iniquity in my hands, If I have repaid evil to him who was at peace with me, Or have plundered my enemy without cause, Let the enemy pursue me and overtake me; Yes, let him trample my life to the earth, And lay my honor in the dust."
Psalms 7:3-5 NKJV

I surrender God.
I'm broken and You are the only one to make me whole.
I can do all things because You strengthen me.
I am who You say I am.

When it feels like I can barely breathe, You are with me.

I'm covered by Your peace.

I am no longer in the grave but alive in You.

You've walked me through the flames.

Now I dance in the fire.

Now I got peace, now I got victory.

I put my faith in Jesus.

I ran away and You still watched over me.

I ran away from You but You never let go.

I may not see You but I feel You near me.

I feel Your loving touch on my chest that You formed.

I feel Your Fatherly hand on my back while I face the challenges before me. You know what I face, how I feel, why I feel the way I do, You understand me more than anyone else.

Nobody knows me like You do.

You are a good Father.

You are a good God.

You are Holy.

You are my foundation.

You are my King, my refuge, my Savior.

You are our Healer.

You are the most wonderful.

You are always faithful even though I was not.

You've always loved me even when I hated You.

I was a stain in this world, but You O God, have given me a clean and righteous robe, a washing away of my iniquity and transgression.

I fall at Your feet.

I bow down before You, Lord of all.

Pierce my heart Lord. Cut through all my stubbornness. Cut through all my mess and pour into me Your love and Spirit.

Break these chains that I have put on myself so that I could embrace You. Embrace me so that my cold heart may feel Your greatness.

I will praise You In the middle of the storm.

Take me deeper God.

Holy Spirit lead me into Your presence.
Be my Savior.
You are mine and I am Yours.
Let me grip Your hand tightly through it all.
I surrender it all.
Jesus have Your way in me.
You always have perfect timing and purpose for all things.
Be the perfect storm in me, causing the evil within to flee and run scared.

"The Lord also will be a refuge for the oppressed, A refuge in times of trouble. And those who know Your name will put their trust in You; For You, Lord, have not forsaken those who seek You."
Psalms 9:9-10 NKJV

"But as for me, I will come into Your house in the multitude of Your mercy; In fear of You I will worship toward Your holy temple. Lead me, O Lord, in Your righteousness because of my enemies; Make Your way straight before my face."
Psalms 5:7-8 NKJV

"Arise, O Lord; Save me, O my God! For You have struck all my enemies on the cheekbone; You have broken the teeth of the ungodly."
Psalms 3:7 NKJV

"You shall destroy those who speak falsehood; The Lord abhors the bloodthirsty and deceitful man. But as for me, I will come into Your house in the multitude of Your mercy; In fear of You I will worship toward Your holy temple. Lead me, O Lord, in Your righteousness because of my enemies; Make Your way straight before my face."
Psalms 5:6-8 NKJV

"But let all those rejoice who put their trust in You; Let them ever shout for joy, because You defend them; Let those also who love Your name

Be joyful in You. For You, O Lord, will bless the righteous; With favor You will surround him as with a shield."
Psalms 5:11-12 NKJV

Thank you for reading or listening to this. I recently started making videos reading the bible and saying a small prayer on YouTube. If you would like to join me on social media, you can find me on Facebook, Instagram and YouTube @christianjameal. I will also be creating videos based off this book, maybe sharing some exclusive stories I haven't mentioned in this book; so be sure to check those out as well. I was led by God to write this book. I hope this blessed you and encouraged you to share your story. Because I want to reach as many people as possible, can you please leave a review? What changed in your life since reading or listening to this book? Also, can you share what God showed you through my stories, testimonies, or lessons? What are some lessons that God has given you? What is your testimony? I would love to share them with everyone in our community and the world. Someone out there needs to hear your struggle and success, your pain and your joy through it all. Please pray about this. Take a picture of this book and share it on social media #GodIQuit. I hope my story wins one more soul for God and their life to be transformed. I am excited to see what God does through this. Until God leads me to write another...

Peace and Joy be with you in the MIGHTY NAME OF JESUS CHRIST, Amen.

Printed in the United States
by Baker & Taylor Publisher Services